Baltimore: Reinventing an Industrial Legacy City

Baltimore: Reinventing an Industrial Legacy City is an exploration into the reinvention, self-reflection and boosterism of US legacy cities, taking Baltimore as the case study model to reveal the larger narrative. Author Klaus Philipsen investigates the modern urban condition and the systemic problems involved with adapting metropolitan regions into equitable and sustainable communities, covering topics such as growth, urban sprawl, the depletion of cities, social justice, smart city and open data, transportation, community development, sustainability and diversity. Baltimore's proximity to the US capital, combined with its industrial past, presents the optimum viewpoint to investigate these challenges and draw parallels with cities across the world.

Klaus Philipsen is German trained, and has 40 years of "on-the-ground" experience as an architect, urban planner and community development advocate. Philipsen explores and compares multiple facets of development in Baltimore with an occasional look back at his original hometown of Stuttgart, Germany. Philipsen connects his work as an architect, transportation planner, preservationist and smart-growth advocate to advance an urban agenda that will propel legacy cities such as Baltimore into the 21st century and the "age of cities".

Built Environment City Studies

The *Built Environment City Studies* series provides researchers and academics with a detailed look at individual cities through a specific lens. These concise books delve into a case study of an international city, focusing on a key built environment topic. Written by scholars from around the world, the collection provides a library of thorough studies into trends, developments and approaches that affect our cities.

Seville: Through the Urban Void
Miguel Torres

Amman: Gulf Capital, Identity, and Contemporary Megaprojects
Majd Musa

Baltimore: Reinventing an Industrial Legacy City
Klaus Philipsen

Baltimore: Reinventing an Industrial Legacy City

Klaus Philipsen

Routledge
Taylor & Francis Group

LONDON AND NEW YORK

First published 2017
by Routledge
2 Park Square, Milton Park, Abingdon, Oxon OX14 4RN

and by Routledge
711 Third Avenue, New York, NY 10017

Routledge is an imprint of the Taylor & Francis Group, an informa business

© 2017 Klaus Philipsen

British Library Cataloguing-in-Publication Data
A catalogue record for this book is available from the British Library

Library of Congress Cataloging-in-Publication Data
A catalog record for this book has been requested

ISBN: 978-1-138-23036-1 (hbk)
ISBN: 978-1-315-38614-0 (ebk)

Typeset in Times New Roman
by Apex CoVantage, LLC

Contents

Figures

Acknowledgments

Thanks to my wife Nayna Philipsen for her experienced author advice and many friends who supported me with materials and provided me with reviews and comments. Among them, Ben Groff, former Planning Secretary Richard Hall, Researcher and Associate Director Seema Iyer, Innovation Village CEO Richard May, Transportation Director Henry Kay, Author Antero Pietila, Author and Senior Fellow Alec Ross, Professor Lori Rubeling, and Arts and Culture Director Ben Stone who reviewed draft chapters and provided valuable insights.

Special thanks to Brough Schamp for providing me with photos from his archive and even contributing custom shots for the publication.

Foreword

Land was the raw material of the agricultural age. Iron was the raw material of the industrial age. Data is the raw material of today and tomorrow's technology-rich, knowledge-based economy. America's old industrial cities are reimagining and reinventing themselves as the nature of capital and labor in the 21st century requires them to pivot from an industrial base to a base rooted in the industries of the future. These industries use genetic and computer codes as their building material, as opposed to iron, and they require knowledgeable workers instead of men with strong shoulders.

Baltimore's story is in many respects America's story. It has a great industrial past and must now transform itself as America's broader economy transforms.

The geographic foci for innovation are almost always cities. Why are cities growing so rapidly even as network technologies allow us to be more distributed, to do more at a distance? Three per cent of the world's population lived in cities in 1800. Today, 54 per cent of the world's population lives in cities, and just 100 cities account for 30 per cent of the world economy.

In some respects, cities have always been drivers of a society's growth, even when 97 per cent of the population lived in rural areas. Empires have always been powered by their cities. Baghdad led the Abbasids to greatness. Rome did the same for the Romans, as did Constantinople for the Byzantines and then the Ottomans. The British colonized and established a chain of cities that linked their empire together, including Cape Town, Singapore and Hong Kong. Today these key cities serve as their respective countries' and regions' links to the world, much as they did for the British Empire.

Cities are incubators of growth because they produce positive externalities, or spillover effects. They allow ideas, labor, and capital to flow rapidly and efficiently. Talent can be more effectively coordinated, and markets can become more specialized.

Can Baltimore be one of the successful cities of the future? Can America's other old, industrial cities compete and succeed in tomorrow's world by being home to the innovations that will produce the wealth and workforces that will fuel any metropolitan area?

Klaus Philipsen answers this question in this wonderful book and animates it with a combination of facts and stories that bring Baltimore's past and future to life, and in so doing, he helps us understand the promise and peril in all of America's older cities.

I first got to know Klaus through our service on the board of directors of 1000 Friends of Maryland, a coalition of businesses, community and environmental groups dedicated to preserving what is best about our home state and to encourage sensible growth. He brought a perspective that was based in the technical expertise he had as a successful architect, but he also brought the broad-minded perspective of a humanist. Klaus brings a perspective rooted in head and heart to the authorship of this book, which I know you will enjoy and find as rewarding as I did. It is the story of Baltimore, but it is also the story of old, industrial America becoming a new, postindustrial America.

Alec Ross
Author of the bestseller *Industries of the Future*

Introduction

Innovation and change must not be done for the people but by the people.

My architecture office is located in what once was the oldest Dental School in the country, that of the University of Maryland. The ceilings are over 20 feet high, and I have a perfect view of Baltimore's Westside, an area that was once the region's premier shopping district and has since struggled to recover from a shift that moved retail closer to the waterfront.

When on the afternoon of April 27, 2015, young people came running down the middle of the street forcing traffic to stop and dodge them, I knew the city had become unhinged. After the death of yet another black young man as a result of contact with police, the city had been on edge for days. This was the day of Freddie Gray's funeral, the man whose name has since become known all over the world. I had watched live-stream helicopter foot-age on my phone and seen how a few miles away things had rapidly gone out of control. On the screen, I had seen the same transit police car going up in flames that had come screaming by my windows only minutes earlier.

I hadn't expected to get involved in the turmoil. Walking towards the running young men to get to my car and drive home, I saw some of them smashing a window of a convenience store and grabbing a few sodas. The group seemed upbeat when they passed me, bottles in hand. I sensed that they felt that finally their day had come. It made me aware of my skin color and business attire and that I may be in the wrong place, so I did my best not to show fear. I got home just fine.

Later, glued to the dramatic TV images of the unrest spreading across town with destruction and fires, my sense of insecurity increased. This wasn't how I had imagined the next chapter in Baltimore's history to begin. I was depressed because decades of efforts that had looked like progress seemed to evaporate that night.

The next morning, though, my trip to work under a bright and sunny sky revealed a largely intact surface, except for a charred drugstore and a few shattered storefronts. A meeting took place as scheduled, and maintenance workers trimming grass and shrubs at Washington Square briefly nursed the hope that Baltimore would simply continue as it did before. The year since then showed the reset was deeper than what meets the eye, and business as usual was no longer possible nor was it desirable.

Hope and despair, destruction and glory seem to be always closely intertwined in this city, which I adopted as my new home after I came here, now 30 years ago, as an immigrant, just as millions before me. Baltimore is unique in its pronounced urban ills located in the wealthiest state in the country,[1] but it is also a typical rustbelt city.

I borrowed the subtitle of this book from the 2016 Venice Architecture Biennale, which was titled "Reporting from the Front".

The US pavilion at the Biennale showed an exhibit about Detroit, but it could have also presented Baltimore with equal relevance. This former "rustbelt" or "legacy" city of the industrial age, ravaged by a long period of decline, finds itself "on the front", not only of the struggle of overcoming the decline and the explorations of what a reinvented city in the postindustrial world could be, but also on the frontline of social justice, institutional racism and the question of whether there could be an equitable future for this city, reborn as a knowledge community.

This book provides dispatches from the ground-level perspective of a "community architect" working in a small practice in which consulting, volunteer work and activism intersect. It describes how the same ingredients that made legacy cities great – connectivity, innovation and a good workforce – can once again become the drivers if they are leveraged by the people. I am exploring what it means to pivot an old industrial hub towards a city of the future with the eyes of someone who designs and plans as a member of a profession that finds itself subjected to the challenge of thinking beyond bricks and mortar.

From Rustbelt to Brainbelt, a book by the Dutch-American economist and former World Bank Division Chief Antoine van Agtmael, indicates a shift from production of steel and concrete to knowledge, learning and people:

> St. Louis, Pittsburgh and Baltimore are former Rust Belt cities that were given up for dead but are making a comeback because their universities were able to remain world-class centers of research. . . . It's no longer closed innovation, it is open innovation.[2]

The shift away from making to knowledge and equal access and the recent new emphasis on manufacturing has implications for cities as physical places. The architect, who by definition deals with people and places, is well positioned to illuminate this nexus.

The global renaissance of cities coincided with a decline of the importance of nation-states. Cities can act nimbly where nations can't. The rebirth of former industrial cities is not guaranteed, even if they have a good DNA with connectivity, density, water, parks and an excellent rail infrastructure. What was once an asset, such as a large workforce and a large stock of factory worker housing, can become a liability if the demand diverges ever more from the supply, the discrepancy leaving in its wake the social pathologies of vacant housing and high unemployment.

The discrepancies make leadership and governance more urgent on any scale. A resurgence of nationalism is threatening the global world order. Hesitation during the unrest cost Baltimore's mayor her job. A good leader seizes opportunities through bold decisions at the right time and scouts for next steps to take. Leaders have to deal with a set of circumstances that consist of demography, geography, history and luck. The Great Recession and the foreclosure crisis in its wake hit Baltimore hard. An overly aggressive police force and a stumbling mayor put everything on the line once again. Now the city could be poised for a take-off that doesn't leave so many people behind.

Baltimore provides a highly pertinent perch from where to investigate postindustrial rustbelt city challenges and create an arc from the particular to the general. Practicing architecture as a white immigrant in a predominantly black city offers vantage points across some of the chasms that divide the American city. It forces consideration of history, race, money, culture and policy way beyond the usual practice of architecture and planning.

The specific tension of a glorious industrial past and a precipitous decline, an attractive natural setting between sea and mountains and extraordinary slums, grit and beauty, provincial insularity and international trade, can-do resolve and dysfunction have attracted creative spirits such as Edgar Allen Poe, H.L. Mencken, Barry Levinson, Frank Zappa, John Waters, Eubie Blake, Billy Holiday and Ta-Nehisi Coates. Nina Simone sang about Baltimore's despair, and popular TV shows depicted it (*Homicide, The Wire*). The national anthem was born in Baltimore.

Once America's second largest city, Baltimore was the origin of America's first passenger railroad (1828) and, after New York, the largest port of entry for immigrants. The city was and still is a hotbed of innovation. Johns Hopkins remains to this day a leader in cutting-edge medicine and research, including a program to figure out 21st-century cities.

Baltimore's proximity to the nation's capital allows it to piggyback on Washington's fame and recent growth but makes it also dependent on federal policy. The city is routinely seen as a laboratory by politicians and the media, who are glad for the escape from the bubble of the "Washington Beltway" to an authentic city nearby.

Race is written large into Baltimore's history. Some may feel that the city's best days lie in the past, but the past is marred by deep injustices that local

Figure 0.1 Baltimore Inner Harbor: from working port to tourist attraction
© Brough Schamp photography

governance, policies and regulations have inflicted on its black citizens and other minorities. Thus, the city is a window for understanding the country.

This book describes some of the recent and current success stories, experiments and failures, and it outlines pathways for a future in which innovation will bring a better life not only to a few, but also to those which were previously left behind.

In a time characterized less by means than necessity, unlocking the power of the many that have been left out for too long is precisely what can make Baltimore a trailblazer for the *American Legacy City* and cities around the world that suffer from inequity and injustice.

Notes

1 According to the median household income per the *American Community Survey* of 2014.
2 Tim Henderson, *Millennials Bring New Life to Some Rust Belt Cities*, Stateline, July 25, 2016, The Pew Charitable Trusts. www.pewtrusts.org/en/research-and-analysis/blogs/stateline/2016/07/25/millennials-bring-new-life-to-some-rust-belt-cities?utm_content=bufferca000&utm_medium=social&utm_source=facebook.com&utm_campaign=buffer

Part 1

How we got where we are

Baltimore's rich history offers a dose of everything: Innovation and procrastination, strife and resolve, prosperity and poverty. This past offers many lessons for a wide open future.

Founded in 1729, Baltimore is an old city by American standards, its beginnings humble, somewhat disjointed and uninspiring, in spite of a spectacular location for trade. If one were to attempt to "Make Baltimore Great Again", there would be a debate about the time the clock should be turned back to, or whether there have been better times than the present at all.

There was no greatness before the American Revolution, just three competing clusters that were the seeds of Baltimore. But eventually, a real city evolved, fueled by trade and incorporated in 1796. A long history followed in which Baltimore was called "a Monumental City" (supposedly by President Quincy Adams in 1827 for its skyline); "Mobtown" for a penchant to riot (a term noted in the *Baltimore Sun* in 1838); "Clipper City" for its speedy schooners; "The Land of Pleasant Living", the advertising slogan of Baltimore's first brewery; and finally "Charm City", a moniker ordered by its own Mayor Schaefer in the 1970s.

Was Baltimore "great" when its clipper ships sailed to South America? When it still had nearly a million residents? When West Baltimore's Pennsylvania Avenue was flourishing as an African American entertainment district? When its women were known to scrub its marble front steps? When Baltimore still had streetcars running in every block? One can suspect that each ethnic group and each generation has its own longings and favorite time but to this day no period in Baltimore history has been an especially good time for African Americans. Class and race play an indelible role in this city's history. Thirty years in Baltimore are just long enough to get some sense of trajectory and some understanding of what makes this city different.

1.1 Population

From rank 2 to 26 and dropping

In the 19th century, when the total population of the nation's 10 largest cities rapidly grew from a quarter million to 9 million,[1] Baltimore accommodated up to 13 per cent of those residents and occupied the second place[2] among those 10 cities, after New York. At the end of century, the city was sixth in size, capturing a mere 5 per cent of this population set. Baltimore retained this rank pretty much throughout the 20th century, reaching a population peak of around 950,000 people in 1950, until a rapid drop in the 1990s. Today, Baltimore ranks 26th in population, and the number stabilized at approximately 623,000 residents.[3]

Demographic shifts also say a lot about Baltimore's and the nation's history and explain a number of the conditions the city has to contend with. As a port of entry for immigrants, Baltimore's growth, just like that of the nation, was fueled by immigration. As the first city with a passenger railroad, with the large plant at its doorstep in neighboring Baltimore County and a host of other industries, it became an industrial power house attracting immigrants and also blacks fleeing the plantations of the South, all seeking a better life. Located just south of the Mason Dixon line, Baltimore's allegiances oscillated in the Civil War, but ultimately, the city became a safe harbor for many former slaves. With about 66 per cent, Baltimore maintains the fifth highest percentage of African Americans[4] in US cities.

In 1959, the largest employer in the Baltimore area was Bethlehem Steel with 35,000 workers.[5] The area's largest employer today is Johns Hopkins University with 25,000 employees, followed by the Johns Hopkins Hospital with slightly over 19,000 employees.[6] In 1990, Baltimore City was still bigger than its surrounding county. By the year 2000, Baltimore County's population had overtaken the city's by a full 100,000 residents.[7]

The dramatic decline of Maryland's largest city and the fact that it was fully encircled by the county without any hope for annexation caused former Albuquerque mayor and urban scholar David Rusk to diagnose the city to be "beyond a critical point of no return" in 1995.[8]

Notes

1 US Bureau of the Census, Internet Release date: June 15, 1998. www.census.gov/population/www/documentation/twps0027/tab01.txt

2 In 1830, Baltimore surpassed Philadelphia in population, a position it held through 1850 when Philadelphia consolidated its land area. In 1990, Baltimore still ranked 12th. US Census Bureau, *Population of the 100 Largest Cities and Other Urban Places in the United States: 1790 to 1990.* www.census.gov/library/working-papers/1998/demo/POP-twps0027.html

3 *The Top 50 Cities by Population and Rank*, 2014 data tabulated by Sandbox Networks as infoplease. www.infoplease.com/ipa/a0763098.html

4 US Bureau of the Census, *2010 Census Brief, The Black Population 2010.*

5 Terri Narrell Mause, A Community Built by Steel, *Dundalk Eagle,* Mar. 1, 2000.

6 Maryland Department of Commerce, Oct. 2015. http://commerce.maryland.gov/Documents/ResearchDocument/MajorEmployersInBaltimoreCity.pdf

7 Suburbs Grow, Baltimore Loses Residents, *USA Today*, Mar. 19, 2001.

8 David Rusk, *Baltimore Unbound: A Strategy for Regional Renewal*, published by the Abell Foundation, Oct. 1995.

1.2 Housing

From polished stoops to boarded shells and lofts

Even laypeople find Baltimore's architecture attractive, although this is a conservative town, and there is little that stands out as daring landmark architecture. In many ways, Baltimore is shaped by how people used to live in this city. Stylistic exuberance was not their thing, not even for those who had the means to it.

In large part, Baltimore is a city defined by its residential quarters and the different ways housing can express itself. Like in an onion, layers emanate from the financial and retail core to apartment buildings and then the endless variations of rowhouses that eventually become duplexes and finally transition to the outermost layer of freestanding homes of all styles: American four-squares, bungalows, Tudor homes and half-timbered houses. Where the better-off trend-setters lived depends on what period of Baltimore one observes. What was once the frontier to pastures and wilderness became an inner-city neighborhood decades later. This evolution occurred in a time when Baltimore could still annex land and expand. After the northern boundary moved from North Avenue to where it is today, "the County" began to expand in the other direction and eventually boxed Baltimore in from three sides. The fourth is essentially the mouth of the Patapsco River, which becomes the Inner Harbor and, finally, the Chesapeake Bay.

When Baltimore was the home base of the Baltimore and Ohio Railroad, there were plenty of rich people in town who built corporate headquarters that radiated solidity and permanence rather than flashiness. They built mansions that were copies of what one would expect in London, Berlin and Paris, depending on the ancestry. The headquarters in Baltimore's financial district, the mansions in Mount Vernon clustered around the Washington Monument, the neighborhoods of Roland Park and Guilford, the brownstones lining Eutaw Place and the streets of Bolton Hill are every bit as beautiful as those in New York, Paris or London. And they were just as exclusive.

Shortly before modernism made opulent ornament obscene, a couple of really obscenely ornate Beaux Art high-rises were erected in Baltimore, one as the hotel Belvedere in Mount Vernon, the other as the Marlborough luxury apartments on Eutaw Place, a beautiful boulevard with a linear park as its median. The Marlborough was the home of the famous Cone sisters who stuffed their rooms with what later would become the famous Cone Collection of Impressionist Art that is now a core collection of the Baltimore Museum of Art.

As a kid, one of my former employees watched the 1968 fires burn from the roof of the 10-story Marlborough apartment building. By then, the building's glory days had long passed, and it had become a place where poor art students lived. The year 1968 shows that Baltimore, like many other cities, was a powder keg, its explosive content the history of discrimination, segregation, and social and racial injustice. Baltimore's buildings sometimes reflect the story of its people.

After the 1968 riots, the fate of the Marlborough changed again. The Housing Commissioner condemned the building reportedly to turn it into a bulwark against urban flight by converting its 80 luxury apartments into 270 low-income units for the elderly. Other high-rises, most of them public housing projects, were erected as postwar slum and blight-clearing projects in the context of large-scale *urban renewal*. Those high-rises became bulwarks of another kind, separating the business district from the rapidly declining inner-city neighborhoods in an almost perfect ring, almost choking it.

Baltimore's public housing goes back to the Baltimore Housing Authority formed in 1937. Its first project, the "Poe Homes", opened on September 28, 1940, for 298 families and replaced 315 "slum houses", which lacked basic sanitary equipment such as toilets or sinks with running water. In the 1950s, the number of public housing units had swelled to 9,000, including the public high-rise projects. At its peak, the Authority had more than 18,000 public housing units.[1]

The fate of Baltimore's public housing high-rises tracked that of similar projects in New York, Chicago and St. Louis. Initially design award-winning for light and air and their solid concrete construction, the modernist boxes soon turned into nightmares, only later to be imploded as failures.

The towers worked as intended when the residents were still a more diverse group of working-class families of various ethnic backgrounds and ages. They were no match for the pathologies that came with the demise of the working class, when they became places of last resort for the elderly, the unemployed and teenage single mothers, and failing from the onslaught of crime and diminishing upkeep. The high-rises quickly became warehouses for the poor, and eventually, they became symbols of ongoing segregation, since almost all their residents were African Americans.

Mostly, though, Baltimore is a rowhouse city comparable to London, Boston, Philadelphia and Washington, DC. Rowhouse facades line almost any street in Baltimore City. I learned more about the rowhouse when I founded my own architecture firm. Soon a small-time investor asked for a set of rehabilitation plans for a rowhouse on Fulton Street right in the inner-city neighborhood of Sandtown. This was my first involvement with the rowhouse and with the community in which much of the TV series *The Wire* would be filmed and where, much later, Freddie Gray would be thrown into the back of a police van.

Through measuring and designing the rehabilitation of hundreds of rowhouses that followed, I discovered the anatomy of the rowhouse.

In recent decades, the rowhouses facades themselves have become indicators of Baltimore's condition: The image of the boarded up rowhouse has become the symbol of Baltimore's decay; the removal of formstone has become a sign of gentrification.

"Formstone" is a very Baltimore thing: It is a thick cement-stucco coating artfully molded to look like stone veneer, including the mortar joints. This treatment was fashionable in working-class neighborhoods right before and after WWII, when many original brick facades needed their first repairs, just as the covering up of wooden cornices with aluminum. The latter was

Figure 1.1 Vacant rowhouse shells in Sandtown
© Brough Schamp photography

depicted in *Tin Man*, a film by Baltimore's Barry Levinson who directed a trilogy about Baltimore.[2] Today formstone and aluminum siding are seen as tacky by many, and their removal is an indicator of gentrification.

There are 16,000 rowhouses officially recorded as vacant.[3] The actual number may be significantly higher.[4] Another 14,000 have already been torn down as surplus in recent decades or have collapsed under their own weight, providing ample opportunities for weeds to sprout, or to have become community gardens, even pocket parks.

Because the rowhouse is so common in Baltimore and because people frequently confuse the building type with the social issues, the rowhouses have also become a sort of litmus test for how people imagine Baltimore's future. *Tear it all down and make it a park (forest, farm)* is the line of thought most often heard from suburbanites who would rather be caught dead than set foot in one of the poor city neighborhoods. *Bring the dollar house back* is the popular request from those who were urban "pioneers" in Baltimore's *first renaissance* of the 1970s and 1980s when a popular *Dollar House Program*,[5] indeed, helped to revive neighborhoods such as Federal Hill and Otterbein. A growing third faction includes preservationists and neighborhood activists who want the rowhouse preserved as an element of local culture and cohesion.

As with the maligned public housing high-rises, it isn't really the architecture that is at the root of the problems and ills afflicting so many Baltimore neighborhoods, but an entire set of social problems and bad policies. As we shall see, Baltimore has addressed housing in many ways, but rarely in a fully comprehensive manner.

Notes

1 Joan Jacobsen, The Dismantling of Baltimore's Public Housing, *Abell Report*, Oct. 30, 2007. http://urbanhealth.jhu.edu/_PDFs/HBR_Index_Housing/Abell_2007_ DismantlingPublicHousing.pdf
2 Barry Levinson filmed *Diner* (1982), *Tin Men* (1987) and *Avalon* (a film about the Baltimore immigrant experience). He later added *Liberty Heights* (1999), a film about the large Baltimore Jewish community in the 1950s.
3 Baltimore City, *Vacants to Value Program*, Frequently asked questions. http://vacantstovalue.org/explore.aspx
4 Allan Mallach, *Laying the Groundwork for Change: Demolition, Urban Strategy, and Policy Reform Brookings Metropolitan Policy Program*, 2012. www.brookings.edu/~/media/Research/Files/Papers/2012/9/24-land-use-demolition-mallach/24-land-use-demolition-mallach.pdf?la=en
5 Baltimore Architecture Foundation, *From Dollar House to Vacants to Value Strategies*, Sept. 29, 2012. http://baltimorearchitecture.org/programs/from-dollar-houses-to-vacants-to-value-strategiesseptember-29th-2012/

1.3 Dispersal policies

From a compact city to suburban sprawl

The biggest hole in the planning process in America today is right at the beginning of it. We aren't coming up with right answers because we aren't asking the right questions at the outset. Planning deals with highways, land uses, public buildings, densities, open spaces, but it almost never deals with people. . . . An inspired and concerned society will dignify man; will find ways to develop his talents; will put the fruits of his labor and intellect to effective use; will struggle for brotherhood and for the elimination of bigotry and intolerance.

– James Rouse, Baltimore developer speaking
at the Conference on the Metropolitan
Future in September, 1963[1]

Housing and the decline of the American city in the postwar period cannot be explained without a discussion of the lure of the suburbs, the dominance of the automobile, the abundance of cheap energy and racial segregation.[2] A similar mix of forces exerted a pull on cities in many other countries, but conspired especially against legacy cities that had carried the brunt of war production, such as Baltimore. Much has been written about suburban life style, lonely housewives, the American love affair with the automobile and the reduction of social capital through suburbanization and dispersal. A smaller body of work has concerned itself with the public cost and economic insustainability of sprawl. Even less is written about the social and racial overtones that fueled sprawl, the exclusion of blacks in real estate (redlining), the nefarious tools of spreading fear in urban neighborhoods through blockbusting and the general undercurrent of the suburb as the place where whites would be among themselves, where the poor had no space, and a clean and healthy life would come from a good dose of homogeneity. The book describing all this most vividly for the Baltimore area is Antero Pietila's *Not in My Neighborhood*.[3]

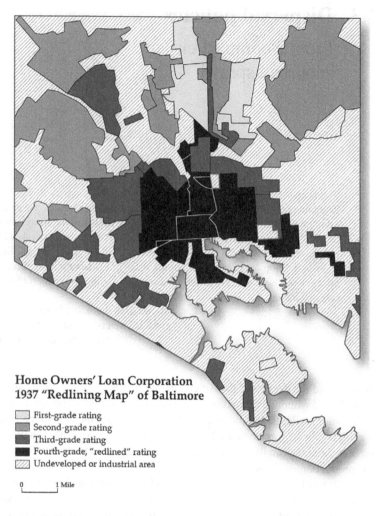

**Home Owners' Loan Corporation
1937 "Redlining Map" of Baltimore**

☐ First-grade rating
■ Second-grade rating
■ Third-grade rating
■ Fourth-grade, "redlined" rating
▨ Undeveloped or industrial area

0   1 Mile

SOURCE: Residential Security Map of the Home Owner's Loan Corp., 1937

Figure 1.2 "Residential Security Map" of the Home Owner's Loan Corp., 1937
"redlining" certain neighborhoods not suitable for loans

© Robert Cronan, Lucidity Information Design, LLC

As a result of the dispersal pattern, Baltimore is a shrinking city in a
growing region. While the city itself lost one-third of its residents, the
region roughly doubled in population.[4] In other words, Baltimore's economic and population decline is not a reflection of a declining region. To
the contrary, Maryland is one of the richest states in the nation, and the

Baltimore region today has an economic base that supports a population larger than ever before.

Yet, the core city in this thriving region has an unemployment rate that is double that of several surrounding jurisdictions.[5] This high citywide unemployment rate is doubled once again in certain inner-city neighborhoods. The dispersal pattern devastated Baltimore's economy: In Maryland, where cities largely depend on property taxes for their revenue, fewer and poorer people have to support the basic services of city government with ever higher taxes (city property taxes are about twice that of surrounding counties). An increasing number of city residents without college education remain jobless or have to commute to the suburbs for jobs that aren't offered in the city any longer.

Stemming the flight to suburbia, regaining population and stopping the financial hemorrhaging that came from a shrinking population and ever lower property tax, revenues should have been a high priority. Indeed, according to a *New York Times* (*NYT*) article[6] in 1973, just two years into his first term, then Baltimore Mayor Schaefer described three goals for his administration: preserving the city's housing stock, stabilizing neighborhoods and attracting working people back to the city from the suburbs. But neither he nor any of his successors ever set an achievable population goal based on a careful analysis of the carrying capacity of the city area until Stephanie Rawlings Blake mentioned the goal of growing by 10,000 households in almost 10 years in her 2011 inaugural speech. She offered it almost as an afterthought without naming specific strategies on how to achieve it or how to stop the continued flight of the middle class. The desired reversal never really happened; at best there was stabilization. The lack of strategy and alignment of all major tools under this goal is to blame.

Schaefer's famed "Dollar House Program" 40 years ago had meager results as well. According to the *NYT* article, only 600 houses were brought back to life in 10 years through the program. In spite of those small numbers, the Dollar House Program left a lasting impression and is remembered as a huge success story. There is no discussion about how Baltimore should deal with its vacant houses without somebody suggesting to "bring back the Dollar House Program". The program had been beset with financial difficulties from the beginning. Initially equipping takers of dollar houses with $35,000 construction loans, federal largesse for those loans soon ran out. Eventually buyers had to fund their own construction, but still commit to completing renovation within two years. According to the *NYT* article, only a few more than a fifth of the 300 applicants in that phase of the program managed to secure the funds. Lack of funds is precisely the problem that prevents a similar program today. Applicants who would be willing to live where vacant houses are frequent and cheap would typically have lower incomes and not qualify for the massive loans needed to fix up these vacant houses.

The reimagining of the waterfront at the Inner Harbor aimed initially to "create a playground for Baltimoreans", an amenity for residents and a valid strategy to gain or retain residents and increase the tax base. Indeed, many of the dollar homes in the nearby Otterbein and Federal Hill neighborhoods saw rapid increases in their assessed value and quickly became sought-after places to live.

The number of vacant rowhouses continued to grow through the two terms of Schaefer's successor, Kurt Schmoke, who tried to bring first-time homebuyers to Sandtown Winchester ("If we can fix Sandtown we can fix any neighborhood in America"). About 1,000 homes were built[7] in Sandtown during Schmoke's tenure, which still turned out to be a decade of dramatic population and job losses combined with record high crime. The number of Baltimoreans dropped from 736,014 in April 1990 to an estimated 703,057 in July 1994, that is, the city lost more than 20 people a day,[8] loss rates that continued throughout the 1990s.

The number of abandoned homes remained high during the two terms of Martin O'Malley, who became Mayor in 1999. He switched urban policies from heavy investment in failing neighborhoods to "working from strength" in neighborhoods at risk of failing. After him, Mayor Sheila Dixon (2007–2010) set on "greener and cleaner", but had to resign after being convicted of fraudulent misappropriation. The number of abandoned houses continued to grow even after Mayor Stephanie Rawlings Blake conceived of a multi-pronged program dubbed "Vacants to Value"[9] in 2011 and made growing the city by 10,000 households an explicit goal of her administration. Depending on which definition of *vacant* one uses, the current estimate of abandoned residential structures is somewhere between 16,000 (city)[10] and 40,000 (2010 Census).

Notes

1 James Rouse, *It Can Happen Right Here*, a paper for the Conference on Metropolitan Future, Sept. 26, 1963, Columbia Archives. www.columbiaassociation.org/wp-content/uploads/2016/06/RGI-S5_1-b4-f4ItCanHappenHere1963-09-26.pdf

2 Garrett Power, Apartheid Baltimore Style: The Residential Segregation Ordinances of 1910–1913, *Maryland Law Review*, Vol. 42, 1983. http://digitalcommons.law.umaryland.edu/mlr/vol42/iss2/4

3 Antero Pietila, *How Bigotry Shaped a Great American City*, published by Ivan R. Dee, Chicago, 2010.

4 Maryland State Data Center. www.mdp.state.md.us/msdc/

5 Bureau of Labor Statistics, June 29, 2016, Baltimore Area Economic Summary.

6 Michael de Courcy Hinds, Baltimore's Story of City Homesteading, *New York Times*, Jan. 16, 1986. www.nytimes.com/1986/01/16/garden/baltimore-s-story-of-city-homesteading.html

7 Terence McCoy, Baltimore Has More Than 16,000 Vacant Houses. Why Can't the Homeless Move In?, *Washington Post*, May 12, 2015. www.washington-post.com/local/baltimore-has-more-than-16000-vacant-houses-why-cant-the-homeless-move-in/2015/05/12/3fd6b068-f7ed-11e4-9030-b4732caefe81_story.html

8 James Bock, City Population Likely to Dip Below 700,000 This Year, *Baltimore Sun*, Sept. 2, 1995. http://articles.baltimoresun.com/1995-02-09/news/1995040037_1_baltimore-county-population-bureau-estimates

9 Joan Jacobsen, Vacants to Values, *The Abell Report* 28, Nov. 2015. www.abell.org/sites/default/files/files/cd-vacants2-value1115.pdf

10 Frequently Asked Questions, Vacant Property defined, *Baltimore Housing*. www.baltimorehousing.org/vtov_faq

1.4 The inelastic city

From rapid growth to a "point of no return"

Baltimore mayors began chasing tourist dollars after it was discovered that the Inner Harbor could attract visitors. The focus on attractions and events around the Inner Harbor began under Schaefer with a series of "grand projects", including an extension of the National Aquarium, a new baseball stadium, a new light rail line that would serve the downtown ballpark without requiring massive new parking lots or road construction, and an addition to Baltimore's convention center that doubled its size.

The big project approach to fixing the city by drawing visitors and tourists continued with the construction of a new football stadium (1996) and two City-subsidized Convention Center hotel projects (1997 and 2006), even though fiscal benefits of those types of projects are often questioned. The latest addition is a casino that funnels revenue directly into City coffers (2014).

At the height of Baltimore's population decline, in 1995, renowned urban scholar and expert David Rusk wrote *Baltimore Unbound*,[1] a booklet in which he declared Baltimore, along with 33 other American cities, to be "beyond a point of no return". His assessment was based on his theory of *inelastic cities* first developed in his book *Cities without Suburbs*. This book proclaims that cities that can't grow and expand through annexation are doomed. Baltimore's last annexation happened in the early 1900s. A 1912 proposal for annexing most of what is today's Baltimore County failed, and in 1948, a state bill ended the city's forcible annexion rights.[2] Ever since, Baltimore was an *inelastic city*; surrounded by affluent and growing suburbs, the city in the center was bound to suffocate, according to Rusk, and become the "region's public housing project". Rusk wrote in 1993 in the *Baltimore Sun*:

> Forty percent of America's cities are programmed to fail. Gary, Camden, East St. Louis are already clinically dead. Bridgeport, Newark, Hartford, Cleveland, Detroit are on life-support systems. New York, Baltimore,

Chicago, St. Louis, Philadelphia are sinking. Though seemingly healthy, Boston, Minneapolis, Atlanta are already infected. . . . The burden of black and Latino poverty is crushing these "inelastic" cities, which, for many reasons – bad annexation laws, hostile neighbors, myopic city politics, anti-black prejudice – have remained trapped within their city limits.[3]

Since Rusk's bleak outlook, New York City, Atlanta, Minneapolis, Boston and other cities have seen incredible rebounds that would make Rusk's emphasis on the geographic inelasticity problem appear wrong. But Rusk's predictions about the concentration of poverty and race remain a pervasive urban problem.

The problem with the *elasticity* theory comes to light when one looks at the "elastic" cities – Columbus, Indianapolis, Kansas City, Nashville, Memphis, Little Rock, Raleigh, Charlotte, Jacksonville, Dallas, Houston, Austin, Phoenix, San Diego and Portland. Some of these 15 "elastic" cities have expanded their area over 700 per cent to capture a large percentage of their metro area's population growth, according to Rusk in the same 1993 article. Urban growth via suburban-style subdivisions may solve fiscal problems, but it doesn't contain sprawl. The decades since Rusk's book was published have also shown that elasticity has not prevented concentration of poverty and growing inequality.

Still, what Rusk suggested to the inelastic cities has merit: "Make suburbs accept their fair share of responsibility for poor blacks and Latinos through metro-wide affordable-housing requirements, metro-wide public housing programs and metro-wide revenue sharing".[4]

Rusk correctly identified the warehousing of the poor as a central urban problem with a strong racial bent: As he pointed out in a recent Baltimore radio interview,[5] more than 72 per cent of poor blacks live in high-poverty neighborhoods, but only 23 per cent of whites do. As Rusk explains, the concentration of poverty is largely a result of the flight of the middle class. In Baltimore, the flight was for some time largely white with the black population remaining behind. The recent influx of the so-called millennials has brought whites back to the city center and the waterfront communities, while now, middle-class blacks are leaving the city in significant numbers:

From 1970 to 2000, Baltimore's total population declined nearly 30%. . . . [T]he city's black population remained steady for much of that stretch, boosting African-Americans' share of the population to roughly 65%. . . . [I]n more recent years, trends have reversed. In raw numbers, Baltimore's black population has declined every year since 1993, while the white population has increased seven years in a row.[6]

Indeed, the most effective anti-poverty program is to help poor people just get out of ghettos and barrios. The suggestion that the suburbs should absorb a larger share of the poor as a precondition for moving out of poverty is precisely echoed in the Baltimore region's recent *Opportunity Collaborative* report.[7]

High levels of crime, unemployment, dependency and broken families are substantially the result of concentrated poverty. Providing the poor with access to *areas of opportunity* remains the toughest political task in America. Dispersal of the poor is deeply unpopular not only with those in the suburbs who resent the mere idea of a less homogeneous demographic profile in their income-stratified communities, but also with some of the targeted beneficiaries, the urban poor who resent leaving their community behind.

The dispersal of poverty model turns out to be as problematic as sprawl itself. It may work in individual cases, but as an urban policy, it doesn't address what should happen with communities from which people have left in droves. One could argue that the solution of high concentration of poverty is not that the poor people should get relocated, but that more affluent people should move into areas currently characterized by high poverty, a policy that would strengthen poor neighborhoods and not weaken them further. Some American cities, such as San Francisco or Boston, had such a high influx of affluent people that they suffered gentrification, that is, life became unaffordable for the poor almost across the entire city. Thus they begin to simulate the European urban model in which wealthy core cities are surrounded by poor suburbs, which is not a poverty solution either.

Some *inelastic* cities that flourished in the last 20 years developed models for more affluent people moving into poorer neighborhoods, like Washington's Columbia Heights or along the U Street corridor, without displacing the original residents. Protecting existing homeowners through limits on how much property taxes can increase is an effective tool. Housing co-ops or community land trusts can provide some protection to renters or provide opportunities for existing low-income residents to become first-time homebuyers within their neighborhood.

The real set of questions, then, is how more rustbelt cities can be made to grow and what measures could be taken to avoid displacement of the poor. How can those cities on Rusk's list of doom that continue to struggle, such as St. Louis, Baltimore and Detroit, emulate the success of their prospering brethren, but avoid displacement?

The answer to why some US cities grow successfully and others shrink is often described as a matter of geography. If a city is located in the historic *rustbelt* ("legacy cities"), it will much less likely grow than if it is located in the sunbelt, where it is likely to be part of the new (knowledge) economy.

This well-established narrative of sunbelt and rustbelt cities and economies has created its own counterflow dynamics: The relative affordability of *legacy cities* attracts knowledge workers ("the Creative Class") who can't afford to live in Irvine or Silicon Valley. Help also comes from the presence of strong legacy anchor institutions that are located in rustbelt cities such as Pittsburgh, Cleveland or Baltimore and lately from the search for "authenticity" that rustbelt cities offer.

The academic institutions were often slow in recognizing that their own fate was tied to that of their host cities. With their help, some legacy cities rebounded from a deadly downward spiral to a rebirth with innovation industries. In a new twist of events, some traditional manufacturing companies such as the auto industry became innovators, and some innovators like Google became makers.

Part 2 of this book will describe various case studies that demonstrate how Baltimore tried a rebirth. Part 3 will summarize pathways and strategies to break the vicious cycles for good.

Notes

1 David Rusk, *Baltimore Unbound*, Johns Hopkins University Press, Oct. 1995.
2 Dan Malouff, *This 1912 Plan Would Have Baltimore Much Bigger*, Greater Greater Washington, March 3, 2016. http://greatergreaterwashington.org/post/29876/this-1912-plan-would-have-made-baltimore-much-bigger/; Michele LeFaivre, *Baltimore Bound . . . The Maryland Constitution and the Baltimore City Annexation Acts of 1888 and 1918*, Independent Writing, University of Maryland, Spring 1997. http://digitalcommons.law.umaryland.edu/cgi/viewcontent.cgi?article=1011&context=mlh_pubs
3 David Rusk, 'Inelastic' Cities Need Help from the Suburbs, *Baltimore Sun*, June 8, 1993.
4 Ibid.
5 Midday with Dan Rodricks, May 14, 2015. podcast: http://wypr.org/post/urban-scholar-david-rusk#stream/0
6 Randy Yelp, Baltimore's Demographic Divide, *Wall Street Journal*, May 1, 2015. http://graphics.wsj.com/baltimore-demographics/
7 Opportunity Collaborative, *Baltimore Regional Plan for Sustainable Development*, Baltimore Metropolitan Council, June 2015. www.opportunitycollaborative.org/assets/RPSD_Final_June_2015.pdf?f306ce

1.5 Coming full circle

From riots to renaissance to riots

On the surface, a whole lot has changed in Baltimore between the 1968 riots and the ones in 2015. In 1968, Baltimore was still a large and seemingly prosperous city with a healthy black and white middle class, but with little change and innovation. In 2015, Baltimore had extensive, attractive and shiny waterfront and downtown areas that could easily compete with the best cities in North America. Indeed, Baltimore was a much copied model with the Inner Harbor and a downtown baseball stadium that cities like New York (Southstreet Seaport) or San Francisco (Giants Stadium) emulated much later.

But the surface was and is deceiving. The smaller Baltimore of 2015 has bigger disparities in health, income and education than the one of 1968.[1] Then and now, whatever was visible as grandeur sat on hollow footings, in 1968 setting the stage for the suburban flight.

Even nationally the writing was on the wall that something big had to happen. John F. Kennedy and then Lyndon B. Johnson had realized the perils of the postwar policies. In response, they embarked on the war on poverty and the Great Society model that infused money for urban renewal and transit into many cities; Baltimore was one of them. But when Robert Kennedy and Martin Luther King, Jr. were both assassinated in 1968, these infusions proved as too little, too late, and Baltimore, along with many other cities, erupted in violence, looting and arson. Some say Baltimore never fully recovered. Certainly retail and commercial activity never fully returned to poor communities, no matter how dramatically the physical appearance of the city changed around the water.

The Baltimore renaissance of the 1970s and 1980s consisted in rediscovering its waterfront. This was facilitated by the local defeat of disastrous urban freeway plans, which allowed historic communities near the water such as Fells Point and Federal Hill to physically survive. Baltimore's new face to the world looked very different than its past image as a smokestack city, but it was only skin-deep.

As we shall see, some freeway destruction occurred inside underserved communities, further exacerbating the state of shock in which poorer communities remained after the 1968 riots. Away from the water, deeper in the city, economic erosion from massive population and job loss, combined with systemic racial inequality, continued. In its wake, pathologies like deteriorating schools, poor service, high crime and bad health went unchecked. Baltimore became more and more two cities, *uptown* and *downtown*, as a coalition of clergy named Baltimore United in Leadership Development (BUILD) came to call it. The unrest of 2015 appears to have been almost inevitable.

What some call an *uprising* presented an urgent wake-up call and shifted how Baltimore was perceived and how it saw itself yet again.

Behind the cover of the Star Spangled Banner with a punched-out star representing the broken glass of a storefront, Jelani Cobb addressed Baltimore in *The New Yorker*'s column "Talk of the Town"[2]:

> The real question is not one of police tactics: whether the use of body cameras can reduce civilian complaints or whether police-brutality cases should be handled by independent prosecutors. The real question is what life in an American city should be.

Figure 1.3 One of the many Freddie Gray murals in West Baltimore
© Brough Schamp photography

Although this question clearly reaches beyond architects and urban planners, they, in particular, may scratch their heads over it. Hasn't this very question already been answered?

After decades of pondering, hasn't a near-universal consensus emerged that the American city should follow the journalist Jane Jacobs' ("Death and Life of American Cities") model of focus on people, not the legendary New York Commissioner Robert Moses' focus on big construction? That the American city should be, in fact, a city for the people and run by the people and not a city for cars and imposed from above by authoritarian planners like Robert Moses?

Hadn't this new consensus just brought about a revival of the American city that manifested itself in New York or San Francisco? This new paradigm asks how well one can walk in the city instead of how fast one can drive out of it. The new, vibrant, "mixed-use" city prefers authenticity and reused industrial buildings, and it can't have enough coffee shops, brewpubs and sidewalk eateries. It must have a funky music scene, theaters, comedy clubs, galleries and art districts to score high in the "livability" index.

What about Charm City, one of Baltimore's monikers? Doesn't it offer many of these things: a creative vibrant art and music scene, restaurants of any stripe and ethnic variety, farmers markets, ethnic festivals, urban gardening, local food and beer? Hadn't it become attractive not only for the young but for the aging as well, even ranked among the top livable cities? No doubt, Baltimore has comeback neighborhoods that are not on the water. No doubt, there is a vibe that feels a bit like in Berlin after the wall came down or Detroit's renaissance depicted at the Biennale.

The unrest brought the question of the American city once again to the fore, this time in the 21st century. This time, it wasn't Jane Jacobs against Robert Moses or people versus cars. The people question came back with a new twist: that of equity. Is this new Baltimore really for all its people? The *Frankfurter Allgemeine Zeitung*, a conservative German version of the *New York Times*, titled their lead story about Baltimore's unrest "A Wake Up Call of the Unheard".

The unheard began to be heard. First via African American writers, artists and photographers that cast a new light on Baltimore, such as Baltimore native Ta Nahesi Coates, describing his upbringing in his city in his bestseller book *Between the World and Me* (2015), writer D. Watkins, activist DeRay McKesson or photographer Devin Allen. Then through the Black Lives Matter movement, and most recently when the BUILD coalition gave the *other Baltimore* a strong voice.

Notes

1 The Maryland median income in 2015 was $75,847, and the statewide poverty rate was 9.7 per cent. In Baltimore City, the median income is $44,165 with 22.9 per cent living below the poverty line of $24,000 a year for a family of four. American Community Survey 2015 as cited in the *Baltimore Sun*, Sept. 15, 2016. www. baltimoresun.com/business/bs-bz-american-community-survey-20160914-story. html

2 Jelanie Cobb, *The New Yorker*, May 11, 2015.

1.6 Transportation

From streetcars to freeways to metro and light rail

Baltimore is where America's first passenger rail line originated, the Baltimore and Ohio Railroad.[1] The city had numerous train stations, and two of them are still active for passenger rail. Today, Penn Station ranks 8th in passenger volume on the list of national Amtrak stations and is part of the Northeast Corridor served by Amtrak, the only passenger rail service in North America that can claim to be high-speed rail. While more people use the train than the plane to go to New York, the Baltimore Washington Airport (BWI) has nearly twice as many passengers in one month than Penn Station has in a year.[2]

Baltimore's port was important for immigration and for moving goods. In fact, the port is actually older than the city. Tobacco was the primary commodity shipped from this port to England in the 17th century, followed by trade with China (which gave Baltimore's neighborhood of Canton its name) and the West Indies. In the 19th century, the railroads gave the port additional importance, and it became a trade point with Europe and South America. The Baltimore and Ohio Railroad also enabled the connection of Locust Point and Port Covington as a place for warehouses and coal transfer from trains to ships.

The port was officially declared a point of entry in 1706 and early on began to shape the city on the Patapsco where shipbuilders settled in Fells Point.

In 1773, the port was incorporated into the City of Baltimore. During the Revolutionary War, Fort McHenry was erected as a defense where the mouth of the Patapsco River opens into the Chesapeake. The fort became famous through the American national anthem, which was penned after the bombardment of Fort McHenry by the British Royal Navy during the Battle of Fort McHenry in the War of 1812, and it is a national park today.

To this day, the port is an anchor of Baltimore's economy achieving its competiveness through excellent railroad access to large US markets in the west, especially for roll-on-roll-off goods, such as cars and bulk products.[3]

WHERE IMMIGRANTS LAND
Thousands of foreigners annually find their way into America through this gateway

Figure 1.4 Baltimore was a designated "Port of Entry". The depicted immigration pier in Locust Point has been demolished

Wilber Franklin Coyle, © Wilber Franklin Coyle, The Baltimore Book, Sumers Print, 1912

Baltimore also had the first electrically operated commercial streetcar in 1885.[4] The city had an extensive system that contributed to the first wave of suburbs, which slowly fell into disrepair and neglect until the last line closed in 1963. The buses that took over the streetcars were another step away from the attractive early streetcar rides to compact suburbs and amusement parks. Buses became the means of transportation for the very young, the very old and the poor who had no car. Eventually in 1970, Baltimore's bus company was taken over by the state.

During one afternoon in 1987, one of the principals of the architecture firm in which I worked came through the office asking who knew anything about "light rail" – everyone drew a blank. "Streetcars", she explained helpfully, and I raised my hand based on my experience in Stuttgart, Germany.

My first Baltimore project had been the conversion of a tin factory into luxury condominiums. I had seen freight trains rumble through the street, but I didn't know streetcars had criss-crossed Baltimore until 1963. I hardly knew that Baltimore had an actual subway line, except when I encountered construction for its extension. I had no idea that this one line was an attempt to emulate President Lyndon B. Johnson's Great Society[5] DC *metro* in the nearby capital. I wasn't alone in my ignorance: There were and are many Baltimore residents who don't know the city actually has a metro.

But the truth is that Baltimore not only had a subway, but also it had developed a plan for a whole network of such lines[6] that didn't look much different from the subway system map in DC. A metro line going west would have been part of a short piece of freeway that was actually constructed in West Baltimore. Cars still zip through West Baltimore on six lanes, but the tracks and stations in the median never materialized.

So there we were in 1987; the new Maryland Governor was the former Baltimore Mayor William Donald Schaefer, who had set out on the grand projects that would cement his legacy. Key was his idea of a brand new baseball stadium to enliven the ailing downtown, close to hotels, businesses and the waterfront instead of the isolated spaceship-like stadium, surrounded by a sea of parking lots that was common then. To reduce the necessity of parking, he moved on a rail study that had been completed some years earlier. In his typical "do-it-now" style, the project was built in record time with State funds, avoiding lengthy federal environmental impact studies. As architectural project manager, it taught me that this region ticks along the initial 22-mile north–south rail line connecting the city with Baltimore County's new job center Hunt Valley and Anne Arundel County's employment hub near the airport.

The new line picked up where ambitious 1970s rail plans were left.

It wasn't so much an integral part of a long-range rail vision, but a response to the idea of a downtown stadium and a visit of Schaefer to San Diego. The old Northern Central rail corridor was an easy route to take.

In 1992 when Oriole Park opened, the northern leg of the rail service[7] was ready to shuttle fans to Camden Yards. The new urban stadium, tailored after historic Fenwick Park in Boston, soon became the model for central ballparks all across America, including Denver, San Francisco and San Diego. The light rail line wasn't as successful, even though it was part of a "streetcar plus" renaissance that had begun in San Diego and Portland and swept to Sacramento and Dallas before it reached Baltimore. Schaefer's version, expeditiously built on old passenger and freight right-of-way that did not include zoning changes or new development, was a long way from the aspirations of the original subway vision, but it worked alright, even though transit-oriented development would take decades to evolve on its own. Except for two small extensions connecting to an airport terminal and Penn Station, it should take nearly 20 years until the next rail project will be on the horizon, a 14-mile east–west rail line. The quick fix approach of the initial line should turn out to be a great liability for that project, as we will discuss in the following chapters.

Figure 1.5 Oriole Park and the historic Camden Yards warehouse served by light
rail became a symbol of Baltimore's renaissance

Figure 1.6 The "Highway to Nowhere" was a destructive fragment of a mostly not
realized urban freeway network

© Brough Schamp photography

Not all of Baltimore's transportation is about rails – far from it. The
"Highway to Nowhere" is a symbol of failed urban freeway policies that
destroyed many cities and contributed to the divide between the poor and
the rich.

The highway not only illustrates the opposite of Jane Jacobs' and Jim
Rouse's notion of planning for people, but actually involves the legendary
Robert Moses himself. He, indeed, had his hands in it when he sold his
ideas on city modernization not only to New York, but also to Baltimore's
planners, who wondered what to do with the various interstates that came
marching towards Baltimore City and would end at the city limits, clogging
local streets. Traffic planners had groused about this prospect ever since
interstate plans had been made. Over the decades, connecting the freeway
termini became ever more urgent.

A key element in the puzzle was the East–West Highway, a freeway that
would connect I-70 with I-95. The only realized piece of the connection is
the Highway to Nowhere, and so it is that transcontinental Interstate 70 still
ends suddenly and unglamorously at a park-and-ride lot just outside of Baltimore's Leakin Park. The connection would have destroyed the Olmsted
designed park and was defeated. The built segment, as useless as it now

is, unfolded significant destructive potential by clearing out hundreds of homes in its path and disconnecting the African American neighborhoods to the north from those on the south. Robert Moses, an authoritarian and, many say, a racist as well, saw an opportunity to "clean up" the "slums", an exercise much on the mind of planners anywhere ever since slum and blight removal had become a legitimate purpose of condemnation and urban renewal. Moses supposedly said, "the more of them that are wiped out, the healthier Baltimore will be in the long run". Well, he was dead wrong.

West Baltimore was heavily wounded by the project, a reality that was recently officially recognized by the Secretary of Transportation, Mr Foxx, an African American who, as a youth, had experienced the impacts of urban freeways in his own community in Charlotte, NC, and where he was Mayor before joining Obama's Cabinet.[8] He gave Baltimore's 1-mile-piece of inner urban freeway national notoriety when he used the road to illustrate why a new federal approach to highway planning is needed. While standing on one of the bridges crossing the sunken freeway, he announced a federal enhancement grant to make the bridge more pedestrian friendly.

That there are only small segments of such inner-city freeways in Baltimore is a big story itself.[9] Baltimore anti-freeway activists had recognized the destructive force of the highway plans early on. They understood that a successful fight against them would require collaboration between the black westside communities and the white ones on the east. A rare citywide interracial coalition against inner-city expressways called Movement Against Destruction (MAD) was created. In the end, MAD did prevent the demolition of 28,000 housing units and saved a number of historic neighborhoods from the bulldozer. Unlike ravaged West Baltimore, Canton, Fells Point and Federal Hill, all predominantly white communities, thrived. The city's Inner Harbor was spared a freeway "fly-over" and a massive elevated expressway interchange. Baltimore's community activist Barbara Mikulski became famous as the feistiest and longest-serving female Senator in Washington as a result of the freeway fight, but the African American communities have not forgotten who got the short end of the stick.

Urban transportation is a reflection of American urban policies: Transportation policies have done their share in decimating legacy cities like Baltimore, from private land developers building streetcars to their peripheral villages outside incorporated cities to car-centric policies that emphasized parking and funded freeways to get commuters back home into the burbs as quickly as possible. Today's recognition that good transit is key to the competitiveness of US metropolitan areas came late but in force. Less understood still is that transit is a linchpin of urban revitalization not only to attract a generation that doesn't want to drive everywhere, but also to free impoverished minority communities that are locked up in the formerly industrial cities.

Better access and mobility have become a battling cry in Baltimore, which, after the promising beginnings of a rail system, is now lagging far behind, especially after the current governor took a $3 billion investment in Baltimore's fragmented transportation system off the table, as we will see later in more detail.

Notes

1 Herbert H. Harwood, Jr., *Impossible Challenge: The Baltimore & Ohio Railroad in Maryland*, published by Barnard Roberts & Company, Baltimore, MD, 1979.
2 According to a June press release by BWI, the airport had 22,761,893 passengers in 2015. According to Amtrak, the 2015 Penn Station ridership was 993,721. www.bwiairport.com/en/about-bwi/press-releases/1164; www.amtrak.com/national-facts
3 State of Maryland, *Maryland Manual Online, Port of Baltimore History*. http://msa.maryland.gov/msa/mdmanual/01glance/html/port.html#history
4 Monument City, *Blog: A Brief History of Streetcars*, Feb. 15, 2012. http://monumentcity.net/2012/02/15/a-brief-history-of-baltimores-electric-streetcars/
5 Zachary Schrag, *The Great Society Subway*, Johns Hopkins University Press, 2006, pg. 191.
6 Subways that never were: Baltimore, *Wordpress*, Feb. 2014. https://transitporn.wordpress.com/2014/02/10/stnw-baltimore/
7 Jon Berle, *Maryland Department of Transportation, Living the Transit Lifestyle Blog*, date unknown. https://mta.maryland.gov/transitblog/long-and-winding-road-light-rail-we-know-today-4
   Andrew M. Giguere, *". . . and Never the Twain Shall Meet": Baltimore's East–West Expressway and the Construction of the "Highway to Nowhere."* A thesis presented to the Faculty of the College of Arts and Sciences of Ohio University, June 2009.
8 Ashley Halsey III, A Crusade to Defeat the Legacy of Highways Rammed Through Poor Neighborhoods, *Washington Post*, March 29, 2016. www.washingtonpost.com/local/trafficandcommuting/defeating-the-legacy-of-highways-rammed-through-poor-neighborhoods/2016/03/28/ffcfb5ae-f2a1-11e5-a61f-e9c95c06edca_story.html
9 Garrett Power, *The Baltimore Interstate Highway System*, University of Maryland, Spring semester 2000. http://digitalcommons.law.umaryland.edu/cgi/viewcontent.cgi?article=1012&context=mlh_pubs

1.7 Making and production

From Bethlehem Steel to distribution warehouses and robots

By all accounts, the history of Sparrows Point dating back to 1890, when it became home to the world's largest steel-making facility, is an American tragedy. The last ton of steel was made in 2012, and then the furnaces went cold, the remaining nearly 2,000 workers were laid off and equipment was auctioned. The buildings, all 3,100 acres of them, were dismantled and demolished.

Sparrows Point and the adjacent Millers Island loom large on the Baltimore area psyche and landscape. These places stand for more than a doomed factory. Sparrows Point was a company town with its own hospital, schools, a store and a railroad; it was served by its own streetcar line, which connected it to Baltimore, while its deep-water access connected it to the world.

In Baltimore's glory days, up to 30,000[1] people made steel and built ships there. The steel furnaces ran especially red hot in the all-out effort to conquer Nazi Germany.

"Making" things was America's strength, even in peace times, and Bethlehem Steel was the proud flagship of this industrial culture.

Company housing was bulldozed in 1972 to make room for another furnace. Sparrows Point had its own port with a big shipbuilding wharf, and its railroad had 160 miles of track connecting to CSX and Norfolk Southern. At one point, the Sparrows Point railroad alone employed 1,300 people. When steel making became less profitable, a cement factory was added that made cement from fly-ash.

The steel plant was a showcase for capitalist America, good and bad. Tying workers to the corporation in many ways, unionization, automatization, pride and prejudice were all part of the story. The mill's downfall came when steel could be made more efficiently in smaller "mini mills",[2] when China embarked on steel production and when the entire United States embarked on deindustrialization on a national scale. By 2001, Bethlehem Steel netted huge losses and went bankrupt. It jettisoned much of its "legacy cost" (the pension plans) in the process, breaking a longstanding social

Figure 1.7 Bethlehem Steel during the last chapter of steelmaking
© The author

contract with its workers, throwing pensions and insurances that had been taken for granted into the dustbin. In 2003, Bethlehem Steel was sold for $1.3 billion, a good sum considering that in a series of subsequent sales the latest owner paid only $72 million in an auction.[3]

Sparrows Point provides rich material for social historians who care about workers' rights, corporate shenanigans, profiteering, and also for those who want to describe the rise and fall of America as an industrial power. The example of Bethlehem Steel demonstrates why today only 10 per cent of the working population is needed in industrial production today.[4] The mini mills could produce the same tonnage of steel as the legacy plants, but with less than one-tenth of the workforce. In the years prior to its shutdown, Sparrows Point had an annual capacity of 3.6 million tons of crude steel, 2.9 million tons of hot rolled, 1.3 million tons of cold rolled, 480,000 tons of coated steel and 470,000 tons of tin produced by a fraction of the peak workforce, but still too expensive to be competitive.

I toured the factory once, maybe a dozen years ago when architects were invited to see the advantages of cold-rolled-steel stud production, an attempt to open a new steel market. I had peered into the furnaces and saw the molten iron flow in large channels. It was a peek into a world many of us have never seen and will never see because the world of heavy industry is gated, secured and normally open only to those who work there. A world of foul air, hissing valves, cranes, trains, forklifts and sweating men in hard hats. A world that barely knows color, and coats everything into smeary grey and black. Bethlehem Steel perfectly illustrates the production world that Marx and Engels described in their manifesto. Compared to Baltimore's new clean economy of knowledge industry, research, medicine and waterfront entertainment, it seems almost implausibly distant.

The impact of the plant on the working-class communities of Dundalk or Edgemere and the entire metro area can hardly be overestimated. Finally, when an investor was followed by a rapid chain of new owners, it became clear: The era of making steel here had come to an inglorious end.

Naturally, the story doesn't stop there. An area that large with deep-water access and railroad connections wouldn't sit entirely fallow for too long, even though there doesn't seem to be a glorious rebirth of Sparrows Point in the offing. The beginnings of new life on the peninsula are simple: a 300,000 FedEx shipping facility,[5] a Harley Davidson training facility, a small shopping center and an automobile storage area associated with auto shipping at the nearby port of Baltimore. Sparrows Point mutated to *Tradepoint Atlantic*. The 3,100 acres are marketed and successively being cleaned up. It could be the most attractive piece of real estate on the entire East Coast. A strong vision and masterplan for this site have yet to emerge.

The story of how Baltimore got to where it is involves more aspects than can be covered in this book. The physical side, although the field of architects and planners, is just a small segment. Buildings, streets, parks and even factories are rarely the causes for prosperity or decline. They are much more likely expressions of policies, cultures and social and technological changes than the cause for them.

After 30 years of experiencing Baltimore as a professional and as a *citizen architect* who engaged in many ways in the proceedings, I began writing weekly blog articles about my experiences and insights, and about what worked and what didn't work in the ongoing quest of a postindustrial city to make it in a new world where knowledge and not production is the key factor.

Baltimore's struggle of reinventing itself cannot be told without an ongoing investigation into politics and policies and investigations into how the city and its institutions treat the city's diverse residents, how investments were distributed and how opportunities were assigned in such a way that two Baltimores emerged: the prosperous one and the one with entrenched and dire poverty. *Uptown* and *downtown*.

History shows that flashpoints of contradictions and tensions often become birthplaces of disruption and trailblazers of social, cultural and technological change. Where things don't go smoothly and steadily, where there are spurts, stops, dead ends and repeated start-ups, is where true social capital evolves and innovation can burst from seemingly intractable conditions. Baltimore is such a place, and it is worth describing some of the spurts, stops and dead ends to find the pathways forward.

Notes

1 Dundalk Eagle, June 23, 2003, via Nathaniel Turner, *Chicken Bones: A Journal for Literary & Artistic African American Themes.* www.nathanielturner.com/robertmooreand1199union3.htm
2 John Holusha, Steel Mini Mills Could Bring Boon or Blood Bath, *New York Times*, May 30, 1995. www.nytimes.com/1995/05/30/business/steel-mini-mills-could-bring-boon-or-blood-bath.html
3 Bill Barry, *The History of Sparrows Point*, The Baltimore Museum of Industry, June 2016, slide 152. www.sparrowspointsteelworkers.com/index.html
4 Federal Reserve Bank of St. Louis, *Percent of Employment in Manufacturing in the United States, 1970–2012.* https://fred.stlouisfed.org/series/USAPEFANA
5 Natalie Sherman, FedEx Confirmed as First Sparrows Point Tenant, *Baltimore Sun*, Jan. 20, 2016. www.baltimoresun.com/business/real-estate/bs-bz-fedex-tradepoint-20160120-story.html

Part 2

Case studies

*Baltimore does much groundbreaking work, but efforts don't come together
as a convincing turnaround and result in a second riot.*

Case studies

2.1 Sprawl and smart growth

Growth management went from environmental protection to sustainable communities, and now needs to add equity.

After coming to Baltimore in the fall of 1986 and taking a job as an architect in a downtown Baltimore firm, the real culture shock came from where we lived. Back in Stuttgart, Germany, I had been a tenant in a four-story walk up with flats. The park where Gottlieb Daimler invented the automobile was a few hundred feet away, and with toddlers in tow, I could walk to the market square past buildings that were easily 300 or 400 years old. Now I owned a Levitt House.[1] The walls were thin, the windows flimsy, the siding was painted plywood, but it was our own. In the words of William Levitt (1948), "No man who owns his own house and lot can be a communist. He has too much to do".

There it sat in Bowie, Maryland, an incorporated city that wasn't even a town and very different than places I had lived before. There were acres of farm fields between various subdivisions, and there was a large layout of generous roadways off some confusing highway interchange that had been built in anticipation of a major university research center, but there was no center.

All of Bowie had no center, there was no *there* there, as I learned to describe this condition, just subdivisions and a forlorn train station that did little to provide some gravitas to this American display of suburbia.

We lived in Bowie for little more than a year, but it was enough time to see field after field being paved over for yet another subdivision or shopping center that wasn't connected to any other development and did nothing to make this town feel any more urban. Sitting on a bench to watch people and their activities in public spaces, a favorite pastime especially in southern Europe, was impossible here, unless one wanted to count my sitting on my bike near the supermarket watching people getting in and out of their cars. Forget walking from the neighborhood straight into the fields or the woods, a practice common everywhere in Germany where people live near the edge of town. Walk access is not only relevant to smell hay, or listen to the whisper of trees. Even walking to a store was almost impossible along the curvy and meandering routes that had sidewalks only so school children could walk to the nearest school bus stop.

Much has been written about the American suburb, but there is no more immediate sensation to what it is than the sudden immersion of a European into a Levitt community. Every single aspect of what planners describe in terms of the suburban metrics of transportation inefficiency or land consumption are immediately and directly felt by the European implant who becomes utterly disoriented and has to adjust life in many more ways than ever anticipated. Moreover, it was obvious how rampant sprawl in the outer suburbs contributed directly to the decline of Maryland's largest city, Baltimore. If the floodgates to the cornfields are wide open, why would any developer or homebuilder try to invest in the much more difficult urban setting?

In 1986, the term *smart growth* had not yet been widely used, but I became an instant disciple of the idea that growth needed to be managed better. So I joined a group that founded the statewide growth management non-profit *1000 Friends of Maryland*. At about the same time, I was also appointed to the Subcommittee on Planning Techniques of the State Growth Commission, which had been created as part of the Economic Growth, Resource Protection and Planning Act of 1992 ("Growth Act").

This act was a tame version of what had been envisioned as the *Maryland Growth and Chesapeake Bay Protection Act of 1991*, but had been killed by local government, banks and the real estate industry claiming invasion into private property rights.[2] The Growth Act of 1992 included as its boldest requirement that all zoning and development plans must be consistent with the local comprehensive plan. Comprehensive plans, in turn, needed to be consistent with eight "visions" designed to guide policymakers in deciding where and how future development should occur. The visions were phrased as broad statements of principle. The Growth Act identified "sensitive areas" for special protection: streams and stream buffers, 100-year floodplains, habitats for endangered species and steep slopes.

The Growth Act had no teeth and depended on local government to apply those principles.[3] To entice change, the State Planning Office prepared a library of best practice booklets and provided technical assistance to jurisdictions for applying good planning techniques. In recognition of its importance, the office later received department status and was headed by a State Secretary instead of a director.

This somewhat tepid beginning laid the groundwork for a more sweeping legal approach five years later when Governor Glendening launched his "Smart Growth and Neighborhood Conservation" initiative. There was still no mandatory regulation and only carrots and no sticks. Only State spending came close to being a stick. All counties had to delineate "priority funding areas" (PFAs), which allowed the State for the first time to collate a statewide map showing where development should and shouldn't go. Glendening's new law became a national model and established Maryland as a leader in smart growth. Once the law took effect in October 1998, projects outside of PFAs were prohibited from receiving State financial assistance with some tight exceptions under extraordinary circumstances. One of the well-remembered examples from that time was the Governor's decision to place a University of Maryland branch in the historic downtown of Hagerstown and not the suburban campus the State University had initially envisioned – a decision that has triggered a remarkable revitalization of Hagerstown's depressed downtown.

The law and subsequent State policies worked on the duality of Smart Growth: incentivizing development and infill in established communities and protecting rural areas outside PFAs through programs like Rural Legacy, Green Print and Program Open Space, a program through which the State bought land or development rights to protect it from development with the funds coming from real estate transfer taxes. It was Maryland's first comprehensive post–WWII policy addressing the uneven playing field between cities and suburbs.

When former two-term Baltimore mayor Martin O'Malley became Governor, smart-growth policies were further expanded.[4] Following O'Malley's widely recognized model of CitiStat, a city-based approach of measuring progress via data, the State began to implement smart-growth indicators. His attempt of coalescing data and policies into a *Plan Maryland* document revived the 1991 battle about State interference with local land-use power and private property rights. Eventually the State plan became little more than a data collection. O'Malley bundled State historic tax credits, Main Street programs and Transit-Oriented Development (TOD) into the *Sustainable Communities Program*,[5] a model that President Obama later emulated on the federal level with a program of the same name.

Through the years, Baltimore and other historic towns such as Cambridge, MD, have greatly benefited from those programs, especially through the historic tax credit program[6] that turned Baltimore into a hub of adaptive reuse projects with innovative approaches, one of which included converting a former grain silo into an upscale residential project. In 2014, Baltimore participated in a national study that confirmed the positive impact of preservation on economic development.[7]

More than 1.7 million acres of land has been developed, or 27 percent of the 6.2 million acres of land in the State. More than 60 percent of the developed land – roughly 1 million acres – was developed since 1973.

In other words, it took three centuries to develop the first 650,000 acres of land in Maryland and 40 years to develop the next million.[8]

The role of the 1000 Friends of Maryland

On the evening of the 20th anniversary of the growth management group 1000 Friends of Maryland in May 2014, crisp sunshine reflected on white sailboats excitedly clanking in the brisk spring breeze in front of dense waterfront infill townhomes. The setting showcased the successful Baltimore, a site that was only a cement-mixing facility some years back. Now millennials, expecting the latest urban chic, could find a home here in a sparkling new apartment complex on Baltimore's historic Fells Point waterfront, a beacon of urban revival. About 150 influential people had assembled to celebrate the birthday of the group that made smart-growth part of its DNA: 1000 Friends is a group either feared or loved across the state. Supporters were here to support Maryland's smart-growth policies, network and sip drinks. Those who denounced the group for having declared a "war on rural America" and considered smart growth as social engineering were not yet in power.

Had smart growth succeeded, and if so, what share had the 1000 Friends? The honorees and speakers were decidedly positive.

"Baltimore is on fire", observed Thibault Manekin, a developer designated by the group as a "new visionary". He meant "on fire" in a good way – the fires of the unrest were still almost a year away. Young and energetic, he showed Baltimore that developers can do well by doing good and that they can thrive on inner urban development. The son of a developer's family expanded the private public partnership model to a public school when his company, Seawall, managed to build a $15 million design school without public funds. (The school system leases the school back.) At the same time, he is developing remarkable affordable-housing projects for teachers.

Toby Bozzutto is another developer who used his dad's company to demonstrate what was possible in Baltimore, first with "New York-style" apartments and then with the wharf apartment building in which the celebration was held.

The last 20 years show an amazing array of legislative victories for better growth, land use and environmental protection – critical area laws protecting Chesapeake Bay shorelines, re-forestation laws, water quality improvement laws, septic bills and stormwater runoff legislation, priority funding areas, conservation bills, better standing of citizens in court, offshore wind and renewable energy legislation – all in all about 60 pieces of legislation that leave barely any part of Maryland's life untouched. In those 20 years, smart-growth-skeptical Republicans were only 2-year terms in power. Was this enough to tip the scales back from dispersal in favor of ailing Baltimore and other historic cities in the state?

There is progress on the ground: Baltimore grew by a couple of thousand residents in 2012 after decades of rapid shrinkage. Silver Spring, once a sleepy suburban center better known for 1950s diners and dry-cleaners than for urban vitality, is now a bustling urban center. Hagerstown, Easton, Cambridge, Westminster, Cumberland and Chestertown all seem to have been awakened from a long sleep. Catonsville, Pikesville and Towson, Baltimore's inner-ring suburban centers, boast new coffee shops, bike shops and bakeries. Transit-Oriented Development is now a transit purpose under state law, and the State is engaged in various TOD developments – more than $5 billion worth of "New Starts" transit projects were then still slated to break ground. By all accounts, growth management is doing well. The fact that those same trends of urban revitalization can be found in other US states without growth management prevents a simple conclusion about cause and effect.

What role do non-profit organizations play in community revitalization, land preservation and smart growth? The group 1000 Friends of Maryland was loosely modeled after the 1000 Friends of Oregon, one of the first land-use non-profits in the United States, founded in 1975. In the 20 years since its founding in 1994, the 1000 Friends of Maryland have contributed chiefly on three fronts: public education and awareness, legislative initiatives and local work through coalition building.

Founding members felt that an organization linking environmental protection with a pro-development agenda would fill an important void in the polarized public discussion, where the world is neatly divided into the two caricatures of "tree-huggers" who want to protect every blade of grass, and evil developers who want to pave it over. The growth management advocates thought that this type of binary thinking was contrary to a bigger reality in which good development and environmental protection could actually go hand in hand. This premise allowed the group to become a major voice in Maryland bridging environmental, transportation and land-use agendas.

The insight that true sustainability requires the overlay of environmental, social and economic concerns is now common knowledge. Many grasp what feels initially non-sensical: that density in suitable places reduces traffic congestion, that safeguards for farms and forests improve property values or that sprawl's short-lived gains only precede bankrupt communities in the long run. Along those insights, 1000 Friends of Maryland built many powerful coalitions in which developers, homebuilders and clean-water and land preservation activists fought shoulder to shoulder for better approaches to growth and development.

Did Maryland's actual performance match its reputation as a smart-growth leader?

The answer is much more difficult than one would think because the alternative history did not happen for a direct comparison. Even without full-numeric proof, it is a widely accepted assumption that smart-growth policies actually changed development patterns and that Maryland would look significantly different without them.

From my work with the Maryland Growth Commission, I know that it was our goal from 1992 onward to have metrics in place that would provide "measures of progress" for the new land policies of *smart growth*. The issue of reliable indicators has since proven to be almost as complex as the policies themselves. The list of possible indicators is extensive. For a "scientific" study, one needs good baseline information and control for other factors that could influence outcomes, such as overall national trends and the general state of the economy. To assist in research and tools development, Maryland created the National Center for Smart Growth associated with the University of Maryland. In 2011, the Center published a report. The findings achieved much publicity because they seemed to indicate that Maryland had not much to show for.

The 2011 report is quite circumspect when it comes to any kind of judgment about progress. It measured smart-growth progress with six indicators, population, employment, transportation, development patterns, housing and natural areas.

For the most part, researchers found no evidence that Maryland performed different than other states. For example, looking at development patterns, 70 per cent of single-family homes were still built outside the defined priority funding areas. Critics countered that single-family homes didn't tell the full story and that 70 per cent of all dwelling units were actually developed inside of PFAs. Still, large lots developed outside the PFAs account for large land consumption outside the boundaries: a lot of land being used up for a relatively small amount of people, exactly what is typically called sprawl.

More important than those strictly quantitative measures, though, is the fact that growth management has done little to break the cycles of sorting rich and poor mostly along racial lines with poor black residents being kept in cities and older inner-ring suburbs, while the outer fringes with their wealthier mobile residents don't provide their fair share of affordable housing or social services.

In the end, laws, policies and indicators need to shift the mighty "market", that is, the same force that brought us the sprawl mess in the first place.

Figure 2.1 Large lot development still gobbles up large amounts of open space
© Brough Schamp photography

The two large cohorts of baby boomers and millennials have begun to tilt the tide towards urban living, walkable communities and compact forms of development. Equity and social justice still need to be made part of this new reality.

No longer can the focus merely be to save forests and farmlands for the sake of the Chesapeake Bay. It is also about urbanity. Having lived out the sprawl model of the suburban dream to the full extent, the huge baby boomer generation rears its head another time via its own offspring, the "echo-boomers". Baby boomers have been used to generating massive trends for decades, and their biological echo is no exception. Millennials seem to have had enough of the dispersion model into which they were born. Aging "boomers" may just follow their kids into urban centers for a last blast of vitality.

Sprawl and equity

The linkage between smart policies and on-the-ground success may be tenuous and hard to quantify with certainty the effects of smart-growth policies, but it remains pertinent to curb sprawl's destructive force, not only for the sake of the environment and a sustainable economy, but for the sake of equity in legacy cities like Baltimore. The concentration of poverty in Baltimore is a direct result of the history of sprawl and dispersal. Smart growth must include end the segregation of poverty, class and race.

The suburban utopias thought out by early 20th century architects such as Frank Lloyd Wright, and his Broadacre City or Ebenezer Howard and his Garden City might have been primarily a response to the urban ills of pollution and congestion. But they were essentially anti-urban and codified by land-use laws, property rights that trumped public interest and the zoning that favored building out instead of up. A systemic ingredient was and is racism and classism that kept poor people and people of color excluded from participating in dispersal. A fine-grained set of covenants, zoning ordinances and financial restrictions rarely spelling out their aim with clarity resulted in new suburbs that were purged of poor people and people of color, groups relegated to disinvested city neighborhoods, unregulated mountain hollers or metropolitan strip developments along seedy highways.

The suburbias of Levittown and its many offspring not only destroyed the natural setting that its inhabitants had come for and depleted cities of the upward mobile and better educated, but also they abandoned a social contract that had been in place ever since cities had been created. A social contract in which government, churches and charity cared for the poor with resources provided by those that could afford it via taxes, thither or donations. That contract fell apart when the better to do simply left town and settled in highly income-stratified enclaves, in which social services were an anathema.

Notes

1 Bowie Houses, Part of Levitt History, *The Washington Times*, Aug. 30, 2006. www.washingtontimes.com/news/2006/aug/30/20060830-081237-2221r/
2 Fraser Smith, 2020 Proposal to Govern MD. Growth Put Off Schaefer Initiative Rejected by House, Senate Committees, *Baltimore Sun*, March 15, 1991. http://articles.baltimoresun.com/1991-03-15/news/1991074088_1_chesapeake-bay-schaefer-senate-committees
3 Philip Tierney, Bold Promises But Baby Steps: Maryland's Growth Policy to the Year 2020, *University of Baltimore Law Review*, Vol. 23, Spring 1994.
4 Maryland Department of Planning, *Advancing Smart Growth 2007–2014*. http://planning.maryland.gov/PDF/OurProducts/Publications/accomplishments-8-years-of-mdp-07-15.pdf
5 *Maryland Department of Housing and Community Development*. http://dhcd.maryland.gov/Communities/Pages/dn/default.aspx
6 Joseph Cronyn and Evans Paull, Heritage Tax Credits: Maryland's Own Stimulus to Renovate Buildings for Productive Use and Create Jobs, *The Abell Report*,

22, March 2009. http://mht.maryland.gov/documents/PDF/TaxCredits_Studies_Abell_2009.pdf

7 *Building on Baltimore's History: The Partnership for Building Reuse*, National Trust for Historic Preservation, Urban Land Institute, Nov. 2014. http://baltimore.uli.org/wp-content/uploads/sites/11/2014/11/NTHP-BALTIMORE-REPORT.pdf

8 Maryland Department of Planning, *Plan Maryland*, Dec. 2011, pg. 19.

2.2 Transportation

Our decisions about transportation determine much more than where roads or bridges or tunnels or rail lines will be built. They determine the connections and barriers that people will encounter in their daily lives – and thus how hard or easy it will be for people to get where they need and want to go.

– US Rep. D, Elijah Cummings, in
an Op-Ed in the *Baltimore Sun*

American legacy cities grew up with good transportation. Their form and density was based on walking and later on horse-drawn transit and electric streetcars. Their DNA largely survived the onslaught of the automobile, and many legacy cities such as Boston, Philadelphia or Pittsburgh never gave up on urban rail transit. They maintained extensive networks, partly in tunnels, even after the first streetcars were introduced. Some large cities such as Columbus, Ohio, abandoned the streetcars in favor of buses and cars, and they have no rail transit to this day. Baltimore joined sunbelt cities in the rediscovery of urban rail transit, but got stuck in the process. The case study of the Baltimore Red Line shows a $3 billion example of what can go wrong.

Rapidly growing newer cities rediscovered surface rail as *light rail* in a renaissance that swept North America starting in San Diego and then continued in Portland, Oregon, and Sacramento, California. Baltimore was an early adopter when it anchored its new Camden Yards with 22 miles of light rail transit (LRT) in 1992.

Baltimore knew it needed more rail transit than one metro and one LRT line to speak of a *system*. John Porcari, two times Secretary of Maryland's Department of Transportation, the agency that is in charge of Baltimore's transit system, liked to say that Baltimore's two lines "fly in loose formation". Indeed, they didn't connect directly, and being of a different technology, most people didn't see them as complementary parts of a system at all. The Baltimore Metro is a "heavy" rail subway system with third rail power that requires complete separation of the tracks from the surrounding city by either running in a tunnel, on elevated track or in a fenced off highway median. The "light" rail, by contrast, gets its power from above and typically runs at grade except at obstacles. Baltimore's LRT carries high over the waters of the Middle Branch and under Interstates leading into Baltimore on a long swooping bridge. Through downtown Baltimore the light rail traverses many important east–west streets, making it very slow. Efforts of programming signals so that they give trains priority over cars have been ongoing, but are inconclusive since the inception of the line. Baltimore's State-run transit agency, which is responsible for all its buses, trains and the commuter service, is perceived by many as a reason for Baltimore's transit woes.

The Baltimore region rail plan and the Red Line

As part of the turn-of-the-century resolve of a long-term planning, a blue ribbon panel of Baltimore leaders was charged to devise a comprehensive rail-transit plan for the region that wasn't based any longer on expensive high-capacity "heavy" rail, but would do better than the existing light rail. The Committee created the Baltimore Region Rail System Plan, a modern and updated variant of plans that were conceived three decades earlier. Through a succession of rail projects, the growing metropolitan area would step-by-step develop a modern transit system that would be interconnected and less reliant on the slow and tardy buses. New rail, the plan emphasized, must be "as competitive as possible with the automobile with regard to speed and reliability". The map color-coded the existing lines in blue and green and the urban sections of the two regional commuter rail system (MARC) in orange and purple. The proposed new routes ran strictly east–west (red) and north–south (yellow) with a connection to the County's burgeoning seat in Towson. The advisory group gave highest priority to the east–west *Red Line*. It would connect the vast federal social security complex and working-class suburban Woodlawn in the west with downtown and working-class Dundalk in the east (the eastern extension into the county was later eliminated to reduce cost). The line would partly follow the same route that had been envisioned for the east–west expressway that had long been defeated, responding to east–west transportation needs that neither existing transit nor roadways adequately serve.

The line would connect to MARC in West Baltimore and at Bayview, to the existing light rail line at Howard Street, and to the subway at Charles Center, which had always been envisioned as a rail hub. The line would serve the new thriving waterfront areas of Harbor East, Fells Point, Canton and Hopkins' branch campus at Bayview with an outpost of the National Institute of Health. It would also serve the "other Baltimore", the heavily transit-dependent older inner-city neighborhoods of Rosemont, West Baltimore and Poppleton. This obvious piece of social justice was not emphasized in the original plan, but became a central topic of discussion after the unrest of 2015 and when politics jeopardized the project.

Initial work towards implementation of Rail Plan began with great resolve and tackled two lines at once: the Red Line and a heavy rail extension beyond the existing terminus at Johns Hopkins Hospital. Political trouble did not wait long.

When the Democratic Governor Parris Glendening was succeeded by the Republican Bob Ehrlich, the enthusiasm to work concurrently on two big rail projects had faded. *Rapid bus transit* (BRT) was added as an alternative. A mild version of rapid bus was implemented in parts of the Red Line corridor. Whether this was to show the validity of the Red Line or to prove that a "Quickbus" was enough to serve the corridor never became entirely clear. In 2007, Ehrlich lost his re-election bid to Democrat Martin O'Malley, and the focus on rail was re-established, partly as a matter of policy, partly because the community showed little enthusiasm for bus and because BRT didn't fare very well in *cost effectiveness*, an elaborate metric mandated by the federal "New Starts" process as a condition for federal funding of major transit projects.

In 2009, Governor O'Malley stood at the West Baltimore MARC station and announced "the locally preferred alternative" for the Red Line.

In many ways, he picked the most ambitious version of the many alternatives that had been studied. Learning from the experience of the first all-surface light rail line that was so slow in downtown, the preferred option proposed a tunnel under all of downtown and historic Fells Point. In downtown, light rail would operate like a subway, but with the smaller trains, it could also run on streets or bridges, a solution that was time tested in Boston, Philly and San Francisco and had been replicated with modern underground stations in Pittsburgh, Seattle and all over Europe. This sensible but costly decision would be called a "wasteful boondoggle" six years later.

Taking a lesson from the initial light rail line's lack of land-use planning, Baltimore's Mayor Sheila Dixon supported the Red Line as a tool of community development early on. She encouraged the creation of a "Community Compact" under which communities along the line would work on plans for their neighborhoods around the planned stations. Signed by over 60 stakeholders, including the City, the MTA, and all major community groups along the line, the compact resulted in 16 station area advisory committees

Figure 2.2 Congressman Elijah Cummings and Governor O'Malley announce the
"preferred alternative" of the Red Line in 2009

(SAAC) convening monthly over a period of 18 months to produce goals,
principles, visions and a set of implementation actions for each of the station
areas. City and State agencies "loaned" architects, landscape architects and
planners as "ears and hands" that would listen, record and then draw up the
communities' plans.

Citizen representatives were flown to national transit conferences to present the participatory compact and meet peer citizen groups in other cities with rail projects. The approach was eye opening at the time and made Baltimore a leader in the use of transit as an economic development tool. The participatory model has since been adopted in many places.

The project appeared to be fully funded, even though the estimated price tag of $2.9 billion was far above early cost projections. In place were federal promises in the amount of $900 million, local cost shares and the state share funded by a set of gas tax increases that had passed the legislature two years earlier. But the schedule had dragged and political trouble caught up with the project once more when a 2014 election upset made a Republican the successor of O'Malley. The Red Line, which was nearly 100 percent designed and only needed construction bids (some landscape mitigation work was already underway), was in sudden and serious peril because the gubernatorial challenger had campaigned against the State's two massive light rail transit projects and his predecessor's tax increases. He would almost certainly ditch one of the two projects, even though they weren't supposed to compete. The second project was the *Purple Line*, designed in parallel with the Red Line and originally conceived to appease the Washington suburbs located in Maryland to go along with the Red Line. The Purple Line had no tunnels and was further away from the Republican base. These were disadvantages that saved it and proved fatal for the Red Line.

In a bold gesture, the Governor made obsolete more than 12 years of planning at a cost of nearly $300 million. He called the Red Line tunnels a "boondoggle" that was too risky and that the State couldn't afford. In short order, he took down the project website and disbanded the design team. Many had considered such an act unthinkable so shortly after the Baltimore unrest that had brought Baltimore's disparities in full focus. Transit had been identified as the number one problem for inner-city neighborhood residents to break out of the cycles of poverty. How to reach jobs via transit in a timely and reliable manner had become a central tenet of the debate.

The National Association for the Advancement of Colored People (NAACP) filed a civil rights suit against the cancellation of the line. The complaint received a letter from the Obama administration written on his last day in office. Whether there will be additional steps is not yet known.

There are many lessons to be learned from Baltimore's Red Line fiasco:

- Large transit projects exceed election cycles and need a compelling narrative across political parties that appeals to a wide range of stakeholders.
- Transit is a convenient political football in a politically divided country.

- The Red Line did not capture people's imagination until it was gone. Its real benefit of addressing the segregation and structural inequities of racism and deindustrialization was not strongly articulated. Instead, the project was projected as a financial and an engineering problem. Thus the Red Line became more compelling in death than in life.
- Detractors can use problems and shortcomings of earlier similar projects and denounce attempts of a remedy as too costly.
- Transit designed not for but by the people needs to be run by an agency accountable to the local communities, and not by a state agency accountable to the entire state.

Lost opportunities are hard to measure. The planned spending of the saved State money on rural road projects is a smack in the face of smart growth and a step back in mobility planning.

Discontent in the rural lands had swept Governor Hogan into office. The reality of actual revenues and expenditures proves the perception that rural areas subsidize the urban areas wrong. Yet, poverty and lack of opportunity in remote areas outside the metro regions does not generate solidarity for Maryland's largest city and its poverty issues.

The unrest did nothing to strengthen the love for Baltimore. It made rural residents double down on their notion that this city is just a huge drain on the State's resources, that the "urban elites" have declared "war on rural areas" and that they "coddle minorities" to pursue a "liberal agenda". This pervasive narrative has taken hold far beyond Baltimore and has become typical for "blue" (Democratic) cities surrounded by a sea of "red" (Republican) hinterlands. The narrative doesn't care about how important those cities are for the prosperity of entire states.

What is next? The access question of the Opportunity Collaborative

How much transportation and access are key to opportunity and how much past policies have exacerbated access problems has become a matter of federal policy. President Obama's Secretary of Transportation, Anthony Foxx, who had experienced firsthand how federal highway policies had marginalized minority communities promotes three new principles for urban transportation, publicly inverting past highway policies. The principles are part of new *Ladders of Opportunity*[1] and are an outcome of Obama's earlier *Sustainable Communities Initiative*, which was built on close collaboration between HUD, EPA and DOT in an effort of kicking *Metropolitan Planning Organizations* (MPOs) into the kind of action they were intended for: They were initially created to address the land-use transportation connection and embed transportation into a larger context. Foxx's principles are

- While transportation needs to connect people to opportunities, it should also "invigorate opportunities within communities".
- Projects need to take into account communities that "have been on the wrong side of transportation decisions" and figure out ways to make them stronger.
- The projects should be built for and by the communities impacted by them.[2]

As Baltimore's transportation history shows, Baltimore figures prominently in transportation injustice. Emphasizing the connection of the disadvantaged to opportunity and the strengthening of communities along the highway (instead of solely focusing on origins and destinations) is an unprecedented, high-profile acknowledgement of the urban freeway failure and a public admission of the wrongs of the past. As fate would have it, a multi-year Baltimore regional study by the Baltimore area MPO, funded by a $3.5 million federal *Sustainable Communities* grant, was completed right in the spring of the unrest and the cancellation of the Red Line project. The equity issue was front and center of the study conducted under the name *Opportunity Collaborative*.[3] The collaborative looked at three topic areas: workforce, housing and transportation over the entire region with its 2.7 million residents.

William Cole, a member of the Board of the Collaborative and CEO of the Baltimore Development Corporation noted in a radio interview that

> the areas we need to focus on as a city are, not surprisingly, the same for the region as well. We have a hard time getting residents to the job centers under 90 minutes, often times we have 'last-mile issues'. The regional conversation needs to be how to create an interconnected public transportation system. Connected places are places where more businesses want to be.

The cancellation of the Red Line is seen by many as just another slap in the ongoing saga of social injustice.

The BaltimoreLink bus project

Possibly to placate the upset residents of Baltimore, Republican Governor Hogan began speaking about improving the State-run Maryland Transit Administration (MTA) and providing better service within its current bus and rail systems. Buses make up the bulk of the service and carry nearly a quarter million passengers per day, far more people than all the rail services combined. A fleet of nearly 800 buses operating on 64 routes (not counting commuter buses) makes Baltimore's transit system 10th in the nation[4] in terms of ridership and passenger miles, far above its 26th rank in population.

The shrewd pivot from additional service to better service was presented by the Governor himself in front of a big prop in West Baltimore, exactly where his predecessor had made his Red Line announcements. In the ambitious *BaltimoreLink* project, the entire transit system is to be overhauled, with priority on bus service. All bus lines will operate under different names and on revised routes from one day to another, beginning on a Saturday night in June 2017.

Overhaul of existing bus transit networks appears to be the latest straw cities grasp to match their dwindling resources with the growing insight that better transit is a must-have for future prosperity. Making buses run better is something that politicians, transit users and advocates can agree on: The promise of a reform that pays for itself through added efficiency, which in turn provides the resources for making buses more frequent and more reliable, is just too compelling.

The premise is that bus routes still mimic the old streetcar lines of the industrial city. The goal is to run buses to where jobs and population are in the 21st century, shorten long routes, eliminate service duplications and spread a grid of high-frequency service evenly so more reliable service is provided to more people.[5] The approach closely matches what only one other US city, Houston, TX, has completed to date: a complete "overnight" bus overhaul. Houston, of course, is a rapidly growing and wildly sprawling sunbelt city, while Baltimore is a rustbelt city.

If successful in providing a more frequent and reliable service for more residents, BaltimoreLink could be an important step in the interconnected transportation system the Opportunity Collaborative had described, even though increased bus efficiency and additional rail service should be seen as complimentary and not as mutually exclusive. In response to extensive community meetings, much of the initial boldness of the reform has already been taken off the table. While Houston's reform seems to have worked largely as intended and resulted in some modest ridership increase, nobody can tell yet whether Baltimore's reform can live up to the promises.

The municipal Charm City Circulator

That even a bus can become a coveted means of transportation has been demonstrated by the City of Baltimore when it began to run its very own transit service lovingly dubbed the *Charm City Circulator* and operated on behalf of the City's Department of Transportation by the global transport and infrastructure behemoth Veolia and its subsidiary Transdev. The small municipal system is a successor of previous less comprehensive and unsuccessful attempts of running a downtown connector service and an obvious attempt to counter some of the shortcomings of the State-run MTA. The Circulator System was implemented in 2009 with innovative hybrid buses that ran fully electric with an onboard small diesel-powered turbine charging the batteries.

The local downtown transit is also innovative in how it is funded: Parking tax surcharges and private donations are supposed to pay for the free service. The funding mechanism is a win-win proposition: Take peripheral parkers to their workplaces and save them money in the process since they can park in a cheaper garage; by doing so, fill peripheral under-performing garages. There are public benefits as well: no need to build more parking garages in valuable core areas. Downtown residents and workers can reach downtown destinations for lunch or shopping without a car. Tourists can go beyond the Inner Harbor, benefiting businesses in Mt Vernon, Federal Hill, Hollins Market and East Baltimore. All with a reliable, free and frequent bus that connects the periphery and the center in an endless loop service of 10- to 15-minute headways. The system became popular and quickly grew to the current four routes with 30 buses and some 13,000 riders a day.

The innovative vehicle, ease of use without the pesky farebox and the real-time app that lets users see actual arrival times soon made the service a favorite of the millennials that began to populate Baltimore's downtown. To counter the perception that this was a yuppie bus, the routes also serve the edges of neighborhoods just outside the central business districts; less by design, the homeless soon began to use the bus as a mobile shelter, further conveying the sense that the system serves a diverse clientele.

Trouble is looming, though: The City expanded the service beyond what its original funding mechanism could afford and started racking up substantial shortfalls in the millions of dollars with deteriorating service. The shortfalls occur while shuttles run by companies and universities continue to proliferate. Another promising Baltimore transit tool is the water taxi. Free, peak-hour water commuter service conceived as an extension of the Circulator bus is operated as part of the tourist-oriented water taxi system.

It costs more than the city earns from issuing private water taxi licenses and from corporate donations. Meanwhile, the water taxi system has been bought by Baltimore's new corporate power house, Under Armour. The sports apparel company plans to run it in an expanded and more robust manner, including demand-based components emulating aspects of the Uber service and custom-developed diesel hybrid vessels made in Baltimore.

Figure 2.3 The Baltimore Water Taxi's commuter boat with the Under Armour
headquarters in the background

© Brough Schamp photography

The cancellation of the Red Line, the massive change of the bus system
with its impact on the lives of so many transit-dependent residents and the
corporate take-over of the quaint water taxi in favor of a flashy service
for waterfront communities highlight the central role transit plays in either
cementing or overcoming the two Baltimores.

Notes

1 *Department of Transportation.* www.transportation.gov/opportunity/
2 Gregory Nadeau, FHWA Administrator, *Press Release*, ASHTO Spring Meeting,
  May 24, 2016. www.fhwa.dot.gov/pressroom/re160524.cfm
3 Opportunity Collaborative, *Baltimore Regional Plan for Sustainable Development*, Baltimore Metropolitan Council, June 2015. www.opportunitycollabora-
  tive.org/assets/RPSD_Final_June_2015.pdf?ae56d8
4 APTA 2015, *Public Transportation Fact Book, The American Transportation
  Association*, Nov. 2015. www.apta.com/resources/statistics/Documents/FactBook/
  2015-APTA-Fact-Book.pdf
5 What Is BaltimoreLink? *MTA*. https://mta.maryland.gov/baltimorelink/overview/
  how-was-baltimorelink-developed

2.3 Housing and community development

Baltimore vacant rowhouses can only be filled with a viable strategy for population growth and community-driven investments in disadvantaged neighborhoods.

The list of US cities with large areas of abandonded houses includes once-shining US powerhouses like Detroit, St. Louis, Cleveland, Baltimore and Buffalo. The list of ideas on how to deal with the problems arising from abandonment is even longer.

The surplus and the neglect are the direct result of a shrinking population, which itself was the result of the loss of jobs. According to the Baltimore Neighborhood Indicators Alliance (BNIA), 8.1 per cent of Baltimore's housing stock is vacant.[1] Research by BNIA shows that if more than 4 per cent of housing units stand empty, a neighborhood ceases to grow. In a city of rowhouses, an abandoned unit becomes recognizable when the front door and windows are covered with plywood: a measure undertaken by the city to keep out squatters and vagrants. In spite of all the vacant houses, the city experiences a severe shortage of affordable housing.

Many houses have fallen into disrepair, have sustained fires, have open roofs and collapsed floors, and some just fall over in a strong wind gust. Others are move-in ready. The sheer numbers are overwhelming: Somewhere between 16,000 (City count) and 47,000 (2010 Census) stand vacant, depending on the definition of *vacant* and who does the counting.[2] In some neighborhoods more than one-third of all housing units are boarded up. In other neighborhoods there are none.

Luckily the number of vacant houses is not proportional to the population loss. A key to understanding the vacant house problem requires the distinction between population shrinkage and household shrinkage. In Baltimore, for example, the total population is 30 per cent down from the peak of 960,000 to about 630,000 now. But houses were terribly crowded then. Today's number of people making up a household is much smaller (2.4), and the space demands of each person vastly increased. To fill 47,000 houses would take 112,800 additional residents, and to fill 16,000 only 38,400, neither number too daunting in a region that grows by hundreds of thousands per decade.

To date, all strategies employed to solve the problem could not prevent an increase in the number of vacant spaces. With every solution, new problems arise.

To fill even the lower number of 16,000 units, the city would need a paradigm shift resulting in steady in-migration that exceeds out-migration – a shift that would make neighborhoods with high vacancy rates, which have no housing market today, attractive enough to growing demographic segments that see opportunity in them. A number of individual neighborhoods have seen such shifts, but abandonment in others only increased.

A citywide shift towards growth must come from external factors such as strong regional growth and in-migration into the urban market. On the neighborhood level, a shift can also come from within via local stakeholders and strong institutions. The shift in a devastated community is hard because it isn't only a function of economic factors, but also of perceptions, social policies and race. Changes can spread from the edges if neighboring communities are on the mend, or it can come from a big catalytic investment inside a dis-invested community that is able to "create" a market. In spite of the experience, "building from strength" works better than even large amounts of money pumped into the middle of very stressed communities. We will discuss this further in the context of Baltimore's Sandtown neighborhood, which was once supposed to demonstrate the latter approach with the defiant goal to set a precedent, following the motto that if one can fix Sandtown, one can fix any neighborhood in America.

Mathematically, Baltimore, located in the center of a region that continues to grow, should stand a fair chance to fill all its vacant units; but the problem is bigger than math and bricks and mortar.

The reality has been an increase in vacancies, in spite of widespread demolition efforts that began to take off on a large scale in 1990 with then Housing Commissioner Dan Henson envisioning as many as 11,000 demolitions in a dozen years. He managed to tear down 4,000 in three years. In a famous Saturday action with city-owned heavy equipment, a midblock demolition unintentionally brought down a party wall as well and exposed the neighbor sitting on his sofa watching TV. Housing subsequently refrained from midblock demolitions. In 2002, then Mayor Martin O'Malley, who in 2016 was briefly a presidential candidate, promised to deal with 5,000 houses through his Project 5,000. Again, the effort hardly made a dent in the total number of vacants. One of the reasons is that even with a relatively stable overall population, demand is unevenly distributed with additional units brought online through new construction and conversion of formerly commercial properties in the areas of Baltimore that have become known as the white L (based on the shape those growing neighborhoods form on the map and their mostly white demographics). In the black butterfly (the shape of the poor communities east and west of the white L) more houses are abandoned. The most recent city initiative Vacants to Value is the most sophisticated multi-prong effort to date.

Demolition as a strategy to balance the demand for housing with the supply has severe drawbacks, though. Neighborhoods with massive demolition look mutilated if there isn't also new construction. Vacant lots don't become elements of a meaningful green infrastructure network without a massive planning effort. City and State are currently collaborating to do just that with a Green Network project[3] guided by a leadership team, an agency work group, an advisory committee and a consultant team, including an ecology expert. The goal is to identify landscape-based strategies for targeted demolition.

With spot demolition now replaced by whole-block demolition, the chances for at least temporary better use of the vacant lots increases. But the new strategy has other disadvantages: It often requires relocation of the few households that held out in those decimated blocks during recent decades. Those often older residents are a valuable institutional memory of the community and a big part of the social capital of communities, which are definitely in need of all the assets they can get. Removal and relocation of residents further weakens the community and likely does nothing but accelerate the flight.

Large-scale demolition programs carry the flaws of the urban renewal that is a stain on the postwar history of many cities. Urban renewal frequently was executed in the name of "slum and blight" clearance, sometimes in combination with urban freeways, such as the 1-mile expressway that cuts through West Baltimore. In the 1950s, "slum and blight" removal meant rowhouse demolition in favor of dreary walk-up apartments or highrise public housing projects. Adding insult to injury, those new low-income projects frequently failed a few decades later and became a drag on the surrounding neighborhoods.

Large-scale demolition wreaked havoc to the social and built fabric of cities to such an extent that it exacerbated the strong bifurcation of the urban housing markets.

The chance that the nightmare of urban renewal or urban freeways descended on a community depended largely on which race occupied the houses. Urban renewal and the term "slum and blight" removal became feared by community and social justice activists as much as by preservationists. There is little reason why large-scale demolition today could be expected to have any different outcome than in the past.

The following case studies show the trajectory of intervention in the last 30 years, beginning with the Dollar House program, continuing with heroically trying to address problems of Baltimore's most challenged neighborhood, the Sandtown community, to the high-noon implosions of Baltimore's public housing towers, and now "Vacants to Value". American cities ran out of steam for the frontal assault on the most protracted problems. The new approach addresses problems from the edges or the proximity of strong anchor institutions and healthy neighborhoods. Creating markets where there were none and privatizing public housing are a reflection of how to do more with less.

The overall demand and supply of housing in Baltimore is one thing. Another is the large discrepancy of home values of otherwise identical homes solely based on location and the racial mix in the city. The drastically lower home values in communities of color have deprived those communities of America's largest wealth-creation tool – the appreciation of their home – the largest asset most will ever have. Depressed home values have contributed to the ever-increasing discrepancy between the rich and the poor all across America.

Also important is the availability of sufficient affordable housing. Ironically, Baltimore's abundance of very cheap houses has not led to a sufficient supply of quality affordable housing. With poverty rates staying relatively high, the waiting lists for public housing and vouchers for rent assistance get longer and longer, especially as the public housing stock is dwindling through demolition.

To better understand the various approaches to address the "ghetto", the housing surplus and affordable housing presented in a series of case studies, a closer look at the Baltimore rowhouse is required to determine whether it is now obsolete or whether it can maintain its original attraction.

The Baltimore rowhouse

A rowhouse is a house against which other houses are pushed so close that they share a "party" wall, and only the front and back are exposed.

With its usually skinny and long shape, the rowhouse is an extremely efficient way of packing much onto a small footprint. In West Baltimore, rowhouse blocks of roughly 300 square feet achieved densities of 40 units per acre, a very workable density even for a big city. The rowhouse is also easy to build, and it doesn't pose any particular structural or architectural challenges except fire safety.

It is easy to see that a house that is between 10 feet and 16 feet wide and often up to 50 feet deep would have serious problems with daylight, one of the reasons why modernist planners with their strong focus on light and air took a dim view of rowhouses. All rooms somewhere in the middle would have no light at all except for the occasional skylight. Even for dining rooms or bathrooms that would be an untenable situation, especially back

Figure 2.4 The Baltimore rowhouse comes in many shapes

before mechanical ventilation or before electricity was used for lighting. To reduce the problem, almost all rowhouses have a rear area that is 2 feet to 3 feet narrower than the front, allowing for gaps between neighbors. If the neighbor mirrors his house on the property line, the gap doubles. This space is enough to allow side windows for daylight in the mid-section. If the rowhouse is three stories tall, such a shaft would still be ineffective. To reduce the canyon effect, the houses step down from three floors in front, to two levels for the skinny "tail". Sometimes, the tail steps further down to a single story kitchen facing the back.

Only the rowhouses for the more affluent are wide enough for rooms side by side; the mass-produced speculative worker house would simply be one room wide with narrow stairs connecting the floors. Some of the grander rowhouses have air shafts going down the center, allowing bathrooms and some middle rooms minimal daylight. To harvest light and air more efficiently, especially grander houses also have pretty large glazed and operable transom windows above highly decorated doors, allowing a breeze to go through the house from front to back.

The first floor was typically elevated from the sidewalk by a couple of feet, providing the need for the classic marble stoops at the entry, which had to be scrubbed weekly and are part of Baltimore lore.

The efficiency of saving two walls and building right at the edge of the street made rowhouses ideal for speculative worker housing common in Philadelphia, but to some extent also in East Baltimore. Cheaply built and mass produced, these gave the rowhouse a bad name.

Thus, rowhouses became associated with slums, crime and grime throughout, from Friedrich Engels' descriptions of slums in Liverpool to Al Jazeera's series about the war on drugs in Baltimore today. But the Baltimore rowhouses come in many shapes and forms and are located in all types of neighborhoods. They also come in deluxe versions with elaborate facades, porches, balconies, turrets, gables and bays.

Since regular lumber cannot span much beyond 16 feet or so, most rowhouses max out around that width, just enough for a good bedroom or a living room, but barely enough to comfortably place two rooms side by side. However, there is no structural limit to the depth of the rowhouse. This simple fact pretty much determines the layout: one room in the front right behind the entry door, which is usually the living room or parlor; behind it there must be a stair to get up and down (Baltimore rowhouses all have a basement), an area to eat and the kitchen. Some of the older and grander rowhouses had a kitchen in the basement and personnel that brought it up into a grand dining area, but most normal houses had a kitchen in back on the first floor with a door to the rear yard and to the alley. Upstairs, one can then fit two bedrooms, one in the front and one in the back, with a bathroom somewhere in the middle. If the rowhouse has a third floor, that allows two more bedrooms there. This simple layout, based on the joists, works down to a minimum width of somewhere around 10 feet wide for a really humble abode (often called an "alley" house, which used to be inhabited by the servants and poor who can't afford to face the streets).

The rowhouse roof is also very particular to this building type. The oldest rowhouses had gabled roofs just like freestanding houses, with the eaves facing the street and the rear. But soon the desire to make impressive facades took over and brought about the "flat" roofs with some slope front to back, thus making the front tall and much more visible. The tallness was further accentuated by a parapet wall that often exceeded the actual roof level by several feet and was decorated with wide copings and large bracketed cornices stabilizing the unbraced parapet wall. Between the brackets was scrolled plywood with intricate patterns providing additional ornament and at the same time ventilation openings for the space between ceiling and roof.

The rowhouse meets the street at the edge of the sidewalk; in better neighborhoods it may have a small planting bed that is maybe as wide as the stair projects forward from the front door. These marble "stoops" are often seen as the defining element of the Baltimore rowhouse, not only due to the clean marble, but because, like a porch, they provide a space where private and public space interact and where community happens. Attempts of bringing the suburban model of the active backyard to Baltimore by taking alley houses down in favor of inner block green spaces failed because people seem to prefer the interaction at the front of the house over the privacy in the back.

The rowhouse offers both the public and the private space: direct access from the street to the front door and direct access to a yard, however small. Nobody walks over anybody else's head in a rowhouse; there are no public hallways, stairways or elevators to take care of; and still densities can be as high as 45 units per the acre.

In the debate about the many abandoned and boarded rowhouses, it is often overlooked that the rowhouse is not only the standard form of living in the ghetto, but also in many prosperous and fully revitalized neighborhoods where rowhouses have been successfully adopted by yuppies and millennials. From Georgetown in Washington, DC to Federal Hill in Baltimore to Society Hill in Philadelphia, the rowhouse has been the backbone of these desirable neighborhoods. In waterfront communities like Canton, even modest 11-foot-wide rowhouses attract much interest and undergo often astounding transformations.

As told in Antero Pietila's book *Not in My Neighborhood*, it becomes obvious, that it isn't the rowhouse's fault when a neighborhood declines. It may have been built by the upper crust and then changed hands over time until it became a place of last resort and was then abandoned. It may have been built as a working-class production home and serves this purpose to this day. It may have been a modest production home in the beginning only to become an object of desire for millennials in recent years. Those histories have happened regardless how modest or rich the "bones" of the houses. Rather than being the culprit, the rowhouse has proven itself as adaptable enough to weather all kinds of trends and needs.

The rowhouse as a housing type is by far not "done". Many creative applications are possible. It gets reinvented in the streets of Denver, San Diego and London. Its main concept, stacked floors and a direct entrance from a sidewalk, can be replicated at the bottom of larger structures or on top of them.

In a world where now more than half of all people live in in urban metro areas, one question becomes ever more pressing: How can that many people can live sustainably? What building type provides comfort, urbanity *and* sustainability?

Case study Sandtown (HOPE III)

Sandtown Winchester, a neighborhood of 72 blocks on the northwest side of downtown Baltimore has become known the world over as the home of Freddie Gray who died in police custody, as the place where unrest got sparked and as a stand-in for disinvested African American communities in cities across the United States.

In 1990, this community had about 11,500 residents, and under the first elected African American Baltimore mayor, Kurt Schmoke, it had become the target of a partnership between the city, community leaders including Baltimoreans United in Leadership and Development (BUILD), and the non-profit Enterprise Foundation headed by Jim Rouse. The multi-prong initiative took Sandtown as a representative community. After Jim Rouse initially suggested East Baltimore as a pilot with Johns Hopkins hospital as an anchor, Sandtown was picked by Mayor Schmoke to prove that entrenched poverty and disinvestment can be eliminated where enough people come together and put their mind to it to change housing, education and jobs. The absence of a strong anchor proved to be a problem, tough.

Sandtown had not always been down on its heels. It was once a well-established white community, and after it turned mostly African American, it was still a largely stable working-class community where jazz singer Cab Calloway grew up and Supreme Court justice Thurgood Marshall went to high school.

The initiative officially started in 1990, with a Nehemiah project named after the biblical prophet Nehemiah and tailored after a similar effort in

Brooklyn. Two hundred and twenty-seven brick rowhouses, most of them prefabricated, were sold for $40,000 even though it cost $83,000 to build them.[4] The subsidies came from a $20 million mixed fund of federal, state, local and church dollars that BUILD had collected.

Federal money came from a grant program dubbed HOPE III,[5] launched by the US Department of Housing and Urban Development in 1992 to aid non-profit and public agencies in acquiring, rehabilitating and reselling single-family homes to low-income families.

Another group working in Sandtown was Habitat for Humanity. Sandtown Habitat was founded in 1989 by the New Song Community Church and had a goal to rehab 350 homes in a 15-block area. In 2011, it had completed 300 homes.[6]

Over a period of over some 10 years, about $130 million were spent on mostly housing. Yet, progress was spotty, and attention eventually waned when the next mayor, facing diminishing federal dollars and somewhat

Figure 2.5 Baltimore's first elected black mayor at the unveiling of 80 first-time homebuyer rowhouse rehabs in 1993

sobered by the experience with Sandtown, shifted his focus from the most impoverished neighborhoods to what he called "building from strength", a triage approach that was deemed more doable and way more cost effective.

The unrest brought not only the neighborhood back into focus, but also the questions why the neighborhood was still in such poor condition and what had happened to all the money. Journalists found some answers in a report that the Baltimore-based Abell Foundation had published in 2013 as a 20-year review.

This question had also been on my mind since Sandtown had been the location of the first major commission my architecture firm obtained through a public request for proposals. I had climbed through hundreds of those vacant rowhouses to measure them up for "full-gut rehabilitation", a term for turning ruins into fully functional code-compliant single-family homes again. I had seen first-time homebuyers move into blocks that still contained several vacant houses. I had seen how often a house that had been on the list of rehabilitated ones was traded for another house because the city couldn't transfer a clean title. I had seen how week after week young black men showed up looking for work. I also sat in the progress meetings where the contractor reported how he had tried to fulfill the community hiring requirements and how new hires had only lasted a few days before they wouldn't show up for work anymore. Time and again we encountered squatters who lived in squalid conditions in those shells without water and electricity or sometimes with rigged up illegal connections. I recall two employees calling in panic after they uncovered a large stash of drugs in a ceiling.

My firm had also provided design services for a small local contractor and developer who was also a Moorish prophet and cleric. He had been first trained as a subcontractor and was then awarded a batch of 10 houses to rehabilitate as low-income rentals. Walking by his side, folks hanging out at the street corners looked less menacing. When they eyed me skeptically, he would announce to them "he is my architect", pronouncing the first syllable like "arch", and there wouldn't be a problem, even when I showed up alone the next time. Eventually, though, the 10 houses proved to be a task too large for the fledgling enterprise; subcontractors, including my firm wouldn't get paid, and some of the unfinished rowhouses would join the fate of many others before and after them. They would end up as ruins with partially framed floors and walls, testament of good will but lack of capacity.

I found at least one of the rowhouses we had completed boarded up once again a few years later. The Sandtown Community Development Corporation, for which we had designed several sets of buildings, completed some rehabilitation and new construction projects, but then the organization ran out of steam and was dissolved.

I heard Yale professor Doug Rae when he came to Baltimore to speak about "undercrowding", a term he made popular for a while. "You can't build your way out of a housing surplus", he explained at a conference held on a Saturday in April of 1997, "that is like pouring gasoline on a fire". Competing with the already existing units causes more of them to become vacant. Housing was seen as a zero sum game for a city that in the 1990s was hemorrhaging like never before.

I saw the public "Avenue Market" on Pennsylvania Avenue at the eastern edge of Sandtown open up in 1996 with more than 20 stalls selling clothing, fresh seafood and vegetables, and I have watched it wither to its current state of many vacant stalls, a preponderance of prepared food and little in terms of fresh food.

Jim Rouse of Enterprise and the BUILD ministers understood all along that for Sandtown to turn around it would take more than bricks and mortar. It would need education, better schools, job training and jobs.

There were employment and health initiatives, and there was job readiness training.

The Community Building in Partnership (CBP), a non-profit organization, was created in 1993 with the specific purpose of coordinating Sandtown's revitalization. CBP coordinated programs for youth leadership, parenting, job readiness, community gardening, health care and recreation and, through a compact with the school system, on curriculum improvements, computer technology, adult education and parental involvement in three neighborhood schools. CBP told CityLimits in 1998 that $8 million has been spent on these "soft" programs compared to $53 million for housing development and rehabilitation.

At some point in the mid-1990s, Sandtown was also declared a federal Empowerment Zone adding additional funds to the array of efforts already underway.

The Abell report shows that there was incremental progress, especially in the rate of homeownership. Enterprise had fixed up 236 houses, and overall, there had been more than 700 houses or apartments built or renovated, many for ownership. Abell compared Sandtown to three adjacent and nearby disinvested Westside communities that did not have the same support programs and found that poverty rates had been reduced slightly in all four. It also showed that Sandtown was hardest hit with foreclosures, presumably because many first-time homebuyers had too tight a margin to hold on to their properties through the recession that followed the financial crisis in 2007. (Predatory lending was a problem[7] all over Baltimore's low-income communities.) Maybe most troublesome, unemployment not only stayed high, but it is higher than in the comparison neighborhoods, proving that even comprehensive place-based initiatives cannot easily address this key factor.

The efforts in Sandtown were not useless, but they did not result in the dramatic turnaround that many had expected, not least the originators of the program. Nor did they bring about social capital or the ability of the community to act on its own behalf without the massive investments of those first 10 years. I came back to Sandtown in 2006 to work with the community on leveraging the Red Line transit project and to work with the community on rebuilding the area around the planned West Baltimore transit station. It was evident that the communities of West Baltimore were still fractured in many ways and were still reeling from the long history of injustices that continued to come at them at a rapid clip.

Reporting after the 2015 riots, the *Washington Post* concluded about Sandtown:

> The most significant problem, according to community organizers and the Enterprise report, was that new businesses and jobs never materialized. And as Baltimore's decent-paying manufacturing jobs vanished – a problem shared by Detroit, Cleveland and other Rust Belt cities – there were fewer and fewer opportunities for Sandtown residents to find meaningful work. In the absence of jobs, the drug trade flourished.[8]

It is unlikely that Freddie Gray's death and the following renewed awareness regarding Sandtown will bring about drastic or sudden change. More likely, it will be a stepping stone in a long journey that doesn't follow a straight or continually forward or upward path.

Case study public housing and HOPE VI

A revival of the urban renewal approach to Baltimore's concentration of poverty and housing and community development came in 1995 when the city embarked on an ambitious initiative to rid itself of all its public housing high-rise complexes on the east and west of downtown. Baltimore's Housing Commissioner Dan Henson had applied and obtained a block grant from the new federal program called HOPE VI. The money was for the demolition and redevelopment of Lafayette Courts, a public housing complex that initially opened in 1955 as a beacon of progressive housing.

Only 40 years later, the complex was reduced to rubble by a series of implosions that were conducted as a high-noon showdown. An estimated 30,000 spectators watched the implosion itself or lined a parade that was held in celebration of the demolition.

How to redevelop wasn't obvious, though. One day the Housing Commissioner called me in my role as co-chair of the Urban Design Committee of the Baltimore chapter of American Institute of Architects

Figure 2.6 The public housing high-rises of Lafayette Courts around 1994
© The author

(AIA) to ask if the group could assist in a Saturday morning workshop with tenants of Lafayette Courts to find a better solution than what the department's consultants had drawn up. He said HUD had threatened to withhold its grant money should the City not improve the plan. This was before the American Civil Liberties Union (ACLU) led six families to sue the Federal Agency for Housing and Urban Development (HUD) to oppose Baltimore's plans to demolish its public housing high-rises and rebuild all units *in the same segregated and economically depressed locations.*[9]

The federal HOPE VI grant was part of the national *Homeownership and Opportunity for People Everywhere* series of initiatives. It had three main aims: the replacement of high-rise public housing projects with low-rise row homes; the creation of mixed-income communities instead of the low-income public housing developments; and the introduction of home-ownership units in the redevelopment. With those features based on a new urbanism philosophy of urban design, the program intended to reduce the isolation of poor residents and integrate affordable housing into the surrounding neighborhoods.

In other words, the program was to undo the disruption from monolothic highrises that turned their back to the surrounding community and had been seen as cutting-edge housing during the New Deal and after WWII.

Baltimore, a city in which public housing agency and the department of community development are in the hands of the same commissioner, was among the first cities that received the new grants, and should receive in the end a larger chunk of money than any other US city. Learning happened along the way. It became quickly obvious that the initial redevelopment plans proposed by the out-of-town consultants did not follow the intent of the new program. Instead of a *New Urbanist* street grid, the suggested plan was inward looking in a "circle the wagons" manner. It replaced towers with townhomes, but did nothing to integrate with surrounding areas. It would become nothing more than a "project" again.

New urbanism was in its infancy, and no development plan in its name could do without a traffic circle and central space, gazebos and other similar basic place-making elements. The new Lafayette Square development plan that eventually emerged was no exception.

The plans got better every time Baltimore's housing agency and its active Commissioner hauled another grant in for Baltimore (Baltimore received six consecutive revitalization grants in six years for a total of $176 million).[10] In rapid succession Baltimore demolished and redeveloped Pleasant View Gardens (formerly Lafayette Towers), Lexington Terrace (which became The Townes at the Terraces), Murphy Homes (Heritage Crossing), Broadway Homes (Broadway Overlook), and Flag House Courts (Albemarle Square). The invitation of the AIA to the community charrettes with the hired architects and the interested residents of the existing developments became a regular occurrence. Just as the outcomes grew, more elaborate and sophisticated public outreach flourished, until the volunteer AIA Committee had become more an observer than a rescue team.

Nationally and locally, the debates about the effects, successes and short-comings of the HOPE VI program continue to this day. In 2010, the Obama Administration began to overhaul the program as the *Choice Neighborhoods Program* with a desire for a more comprehensive approach also visible in the administration's Livable Communities Initiative,[11] in which HUD, EPA and DOT collaborate to address neighborhoods in the context of housing, environmental issues and transportation.

The Baltimore redevelopments had 30 per cent fewer residents simply by reducing density. The displacement of so many people may have individually opened new opportunities for the relocated families (one of the objectives), but it inflicted once again what New York–based research psychiatrist Mindy Thompson Fullilove has termed "root shock", the trauma of having to leave ones community.[12] The mass relocation also impacted nearby retail and services, especially on the westside where the loss was initially not compensated by other new development.

The number of affordable low-income rental units was reduced even more (for example for Lexington Terrace and Murphy Homes from 1,448 to just 325 (plus 325 affordable for-sale units).[13] This was good for maintaining an income diverse community with affordable and market-rate rental units and ownership homes, but since those affordable units were not replaced elsewhere, HOPE VI exacerbated the citywide deficit of affordable units. Tenants equipped with *Section 8* housing vouchers moved to neighborhoods with relatively better opportunities; however, some of those were in a state of fragile balance. This set off the familiar efforts of keeping poor people of color out. The ACLU observes:

> If ability to pay determined where the low-income families in the region lived, whites and blacks alike would be concentrated in low-income city neighborhoods. However, most low-income whites (60%) live throughout Baltimore's suburbs and enjoy the advantages of suburban schools and job opportunities. But 86% of low-income African Americans are concentrated in Baltimore City.[14]

The initial redevelopments were so low density that they looked like the suburbs had come to Baltimore. Importing suburban design has been a re-occurring "strategy" as if Baltimore wouldn't have enough freestanding homes with yards and garages in its peripheral neighborhoods. A low-density suburban layout for developments immediately adjacent to downtown is not new urbanism. It wastes the potential of valuable locations with great access and is also in conflict with the New Urbanist concept of the *transect* in which density gradually decreases from the center to the periphery.

Most satisfying in terms of urban design is the Albemarle Square redevelopment, which included a smattering of mixed use and building types more appropriate so close to downtown. All projects were successful in the initial absorption of all components of offered housing, including the market rate and for sale units. However, the two projects on the westside, Lexington

Terrace and Heritage Crossing, suffer from the fact that plans to spruce up adjacent quarters have not materialized.

Was dynamite really the only possible answer to the failed public housing high-rises?

These were buildings that had won design awards only 50 years ago. Solid concrete and brick had once replaced dilapidated "slums" of presumably shoddy rowhouses. Dynamite reduced them to rubble. Ironically, they were then replaced once again by flimsy rowhouses constructed of 2″ × 4″ wood frames, gypsum, plywood, vinyl siding and asphalt shingles. Couldn't the old concrete high-rises have been rehabilitated as retirement homes or residences for childless urban dwellers? Wouldn't there have been a way to mitigate their anti-urban layout through appropriate infill? The double demolition conceals the deeper underlying failures that led to slums and warehousing of the poor in the first place. It was not so much the buildings that failed as the national and local housing policies. Housing policy was also at the heart of the ACLU's landmark lawsuit against HUD. In the case of *Thompson vs. HUD*, six Baltimore families filed on behalf of 14,000 other low-income families, alleging that the HUD program intended to rebuild all units in the same segregated, economically depressed locations in which the demolition of the housing projects occurred. In 1996, a year after the filing, *Thompson vs. HUD* produced a consent decree between the families and the government, calling for 3,000 new housing opportunities for public housing families, including the redevelopment of the high-rise sites.

The problems with public housing are far from resolved, at the national level and in Baltimore. In spite of a drastically reduced public housing stock, Baltimore Housing, the City's two-task housing agency, which does community development and manages the City-owned public housing units, has fallen far behind in maintenance of the remaining units. In that, it is just like its sister agencies in New York or many other cities that saw reduced federal funds coming in, while facing a growing need for public housing with fewer units at hand. By now, public housing is synonymous with a place of last resort.

The rental assistance program

Another remedy to prop up affordable-housing stock that HUD has devised under the Obama Administration is the Rental Assistance Demonstration Program (RAD). Once again, Baltimore is an early adopter and has participated in the program from the start. Under RAD, HUD-restricted housing units essentially are transferred into the ownership of a housing authority or the private entity that held the units before. Under the new procedure, project-based subsidies transfer to private entities, which can operate free from a number of restrictions housing authorities had to follow, including which funds can be used for renovations. The idea is that this will facilitate dealing with the backlog of repairs through the use of private financing sources, without increasing HUD's budget. Subsidies for the entire portfolio of the Housing Authority are transformed into project-specific subsidies. Several municipal housing agencies are in the process of divesting themselves from all publicly owned units; others, like Baltimore, are trying to sell large, hard-to-manage projects to accumulate funds. It remains to be seen if the magic trick of leveraging private capital will actually work without decreasing access to affordable housing compared to current levels. The possible problem wouldn't be a decrease in the number of affordable units, but the possibility that the voucher funds will be insufficient to fill all units, especially if *Moving to Opportunity*[15] will be supported by increasing voucher money for units located in higher-rent areas.

A predecessor to RAD was a joint venture partnership in which the housing authority also divested itself from ill-maintained, scattered site public housing units by partnering with a private developer and the community in a "develop, own and manage" approach that allowed "full-gut rehabilitation" of 23 units and the construction of 8 additional affordable units on City-owned land. This small model allowed to maintain the affordability and the participation of the local African American Community of Sharp Leadenhall in some of the rent proceeds in a long-term agreement. My firm ArchPlan was the architect for the project.

Case study: vacants to value

> *Fixing what's broken in Baltimore requires that we address the sea of aban-*
> *doned, dilapidated buildings that are infecting entire neighborhoods. . . .*
> *They aren't just unsightly, they are also unsafe, unhealthy and a hotbed*
> *for crime.*
>
> —*Governor Hogan*[16]

The vexing problem of Baltimore's vacant housing has kept many Baltimore Housing Commissioners busy. In 2010, Baltimore unveiled the latest program under the catchy name "Vacants to Value" or V2V. No longer was this a program that scattered demolition and rehabilitation all over the place. By now, the process of getting a clear title to abandoned buildings and lots was streamlined, and census tracts were grouped by market strength. Demolition was to occur in communities in severe distress where there was no market, while redevelopment or rehabilitation was to concentrate in areas with emerging markets and on a scale to make a difference.

The market classification brought sobering results: Only 86 of 250 neighborhoods were targeted for renovation. Twelve thousand of the officially recognized 16,000 vacant homes are located in "stressed markets", that is, neighborhoods not targeted for value creation for the absence of any market. This still leaves a large emphasis on demolition.

In 2015, at the fifth anniversary of the V2V program, Baltimore Housing conducted a "summit" at the Baltimore Convention Center, marketing the program to investors, developers and community members.

Julia Day, Deputy Commissioner at Housing and responsible for Land Resources, said that "residents are clamoring to be relocated from dilapidated blocks". The Commissioner himself intoned that "blight elimination was just the tag line, the bottom line is people".[17] Bus tours were available under the name "Beyond the Wire", a reference to the infamous TV series that played in Baltimore's Sandtown neighborhood.

Again, the Abell Foundation analyzed how the program had performed.[18] Its report came to less rousing conclusions than the Housing Department; nevertheless, the program was considered somewhat successful. The report states that

> Vacants to Value is a dependable system for identifying and cracking down on owners of derelict houses in scarred neighborhoods with plummeting property values. The program is showing signs of success in rejuvenating neighborhoods that were long neglected, like Oliver, McElderry Park, and Greenmount West, even though these neighborhoods benefited also from other funds and programs.

They are instructive in terms how successful renewal can be done.

The story of Greenmount West and Oliver represents several lessons learned from Sandtown that were well explained at the summit by Sean Closkey, President of TRF Redevelopment Partners.[19] In a workshop, he outlined the strategies for the two eastside communities in very clear language:

> People may see [the vacant houses] as a vacancy problem but it is an economic problem. The only way it can be reversed it is to get the private sector engaged. There must be a scale and a sequence to intervention.[20]

In the target communities, he mentioned a drop from 895 vacant structures to 478. He spoke of "catalytic investments" that were made with investment funds and by the non-profits in the partnership (TRF raised and invested

Figure 2.7 Station North: Artists as pioneers with live-work units in new town
houses and the City Arts building in the background

© The author

$65 million in Baltimore), "after which non-profits need to fade out and for-profits need to come in". He said, "Don't chase the price. Offer something you don't get elsewhere in the city". All the Greenmount West "disposition houses" (houses the City had offered for development) were sold.

The TRF presentation was followed up by one of the market-rate housing developers who stepped in to rehabilitate 75 houses in Oliver. This is a neighborhood that was extremely disinvested and had garnered attention after an entire family of a mother and five children had been firebombed and killed for cooperating with police.[21] The developer noted how TRF supported him with know-how and how they had created the market he now works in.

The Hopkins biopark development

John Lecker, corporate speaker and Vice President of Forest City, looked a bit out of place in the art bar Windup Space on North Avenue. He had a drink before he gave his talk. "A first", he said, "I will be back for sure". "Design

Conversation #51" explored "alternative ways of funding development through crowd sourcing".[22] Crowd-funded development on Washington's H Street and a Kickstarter campaign for African library modules were the other presentations.

The development Lecker presented was neither crowd sourced nor does he usually speak in front of community activists, artists, designers and architects as assembled here. Lecker may not be used to applause since the Forest City–led redevelopment of 88 acres of land immediately north of the world-famous Johns Hopkins Hospital in East Baltimore in a neighborhood once called Middle East is still controversial. But here in 2015 at the Windup Space, his many cold numbers he served in rapid fire were warmly received: 731 households relocated, $187 million in contracts so far, 37 per cent MBE participation, 40 rehabs, 1,500 parking spaces, 280,000 square feet of retail, 321 student housing units, 6-acre park.

To re-invent the Middle East by rebuilding the entire community in tandem with the creation of a bio-technology park was not something the community had asked for. It was much more urban renewal than crowd sourcing. It came about under then-Mayor Martin O'Malley's policy of "building from strength": Make a neighborhood whole again by expanding the strength of an existing asset rather than creating an asset from the ground up. The biopark initiative intended to build from the strength of one of the best-known anchor institutions worldwide: the Johns Hopkins Hospital. However, it did so in one of the most dis-invested and devastated neighborhoods in Baltimore in an open-heart-surgery approach, once again reminiscent of old-style urban renewal. The project picked up on Jim Rouse's initial intention before Mayor Schmoke had talked him into Sandtown Winchester as the place where the vision for a prototype of urban re-investment should be carried out.

Thirteen years after the Hopkins biotech initiative started in 2002, and more than 25 years after Rouse started his work in Sandtown, the more dramatic change can, no doubt, be found north of Hopkins.

Yet today, neither residents nor businesses follow this experiment with particular interest. Even the quasi-governmental East Baltimore Development Inc. (EBDI) calls it "the largest redevelopment in America" on its own website. Press reports have been largely negative, especially a series by the local *Daily Record* titled "A Dream Derailed", but the project quietly proceeds neither derailing in scandal nor becoming the shining beacon originally envisioned.

The event at the Windup showed that the undertaking is ready to re-invent itself and come across not as the heavy-handed government initiated injustice as which many saw it initially but as a model for an urban re-charge carried out not to carry a favor for the anchor institution Johns Hopkins but as an engagement by a multitude of non-profits and for-profits. EBDI has taken a back seat behind the non-profit Casey Foundation and the for-profit developer Forest City. Both appear to be engaged not for the quick buck but the long haul of creating a real community.

The story of EBDI is so complex and branched out that it is impossible to fully retell it in the space of this book, even though I have been around for most of the journey.

For example, in June of 2002, I sat among 500 East Baltimore residents in the auditorium of Dunbar High at one of the initial hearings that had been set forth by the City in the course of amending and collapsing several urban renewal ordinances in effect in the area. The battle lines had already been drawn between a number of groups: (1) representatives of the "Save Middle East Action Coalition", who were opposed to urban renewal, (2) residents who welcomed the change, (3) those who wouldn't want to move, (4) those who wanted more relocation money than was initially offered and (5) those who insisted on free choice of where to relocate, as the Fair Housing Act provides, rather than only within the City limits as officials had envisioned. The meeting was heated, the testimony was long, but in the end, there was no revolution. To navigate these treacherous waters, Council member Paula Branch Johnson had assembled a group of people as advisers, and I was one of them representing the AIA. We prepared and submitted a set of principles for the process that suggested rules for design, relocation, transportation and preservation. We proposed less parking, more open space and a commercial node. Much of this made it into the actual process that started out with charrettes and plans prepared by *Urban Design Associates* of Pittsburgh. Nobody back then thought that 11 years later EBDI would still be only in the first half of its overall development and would have tossed out at least two masterplans.

I was also around in May 2006 as part of a set of consultants who were sitting in a gym around tables each with about 10 residents for another charrette and another set of planners. This time it was Sasaki of Watertown near Boston, and ArchPlan was a subconsultant most responsible for the preservation element.

EBDI Director Jack Shannon opened the event saying,

> We must not repeat the mistakes made of the previous charrette process. While I was not here, from everything I have heard, it was a flawed process. You came to the meetings and a plan was rolled out without listening to you and to your ideas. We know that you are the true experts in this community and we want your ideas to ensure the best plan can be created for you, your families and the neighborhood. Many of you have been here for 20+ years – we must learn from you regarding what will work and what won't work in this community.[23]

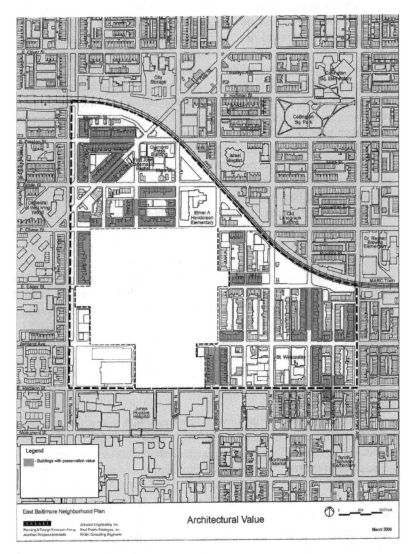

Figure 2.8 The redevelopment area north of Johns Hopkins Hospital with the demolition area (white) and preservation blocks (darker shade building rows)

© The author

It wasn't the last time that EBDI had to be contrite, and this second visioning process would still only become the base for the selection of a master developer. But step by step, many community goals and ideas found their way into the blueprints and programs that were rolled out.

ArchPlan was once again engaged in 2010 when my office, along with two other local firms, assisted long-time East Baltimore homeowners in defining how they would like their rowhouses to be rehabilitated. Those mostly elderly residents had stuck it out in the community through decades, including those when their neighborhood dwindled and almost disappeared. Now, they could describe their wishes and apply pretty much the same funds for the renovation of their modest houses that others had received for relocation homes outside of East Baltimore. Although the 40 homes that were refurbished pale in comparison to the many more that were demolished or whose residents were relocated, retaining at least some of the original residents was an important step towards keeping some of the "social capital" intact without which no community can thrive and any promise of diversity would be nothing but lip service.

The project had started out like so many other urban renewals: too many residents relocated and too much demolition. In phase one, every single home was demolished until the neighborhood, called Middle East for its location in the city, looked like a war zone. Compensation and mitigation were fought over each step of the way: Relocated residents received first rights of refusal on the new tenements, and eventually residents who wanted to stay in the community could use the relocation money for rehabilitation. Some big ideas stuck, some remained unfulfilled.

Although an envisioned commuter rail transit stop along the existing Marc train line is still a paper dream, a brand new school is complete and operating. This school is a $42 million, 90,000-square-foot facility on a 7-acre campus, shared with a $10 million, 28,000-square-foot early childhood center.

The masterplan was refined every few years with a new set of consultants. In a third and, so far, final revision of the masterplan undertaken by the master-developer Forest City, a large urban park was introduced as the centerpiece of the redevelopment. Additional players came, such as the Baltimore rising star the Maryland College of Art (MICA), which opened a branch facility for its community-based social design in a former church facility. The public Northeast market nearby was renovated, and a 20-story student housing project is already completed. The 31-acre biotech park morphed into the 1.1-million-square-foot Science and Technology Park with a number of facility buildings completed along with parking garages and restaurants.

In the transition from the ambitious Jack Shannon as the CEO of EBDI to the more laid back Chris Shea, EBDI changed from a group that tried to organize and control everything to a group that wants to delegate as much as possible to other entities. Johns Hopkins has learned to listen better to the community that long eyed it with great suspicion as the "castle on the hill". The Casey Foundation, which for a long time has been the only group putting large funds up to soften the impacts of this urban renewal, is now joined by others funding community-oriented work. Community hiring, community participation and partnerships have been refined and improved to a point that many approaches tested here can now serve as models elsewhere in the city.

Ultimately, the success of the 88-acre EBDI initiative and the hundreds of millions of dollars of public investment will depend on what happens in the areas beyond "piano", the moniker used to describe the planning area due to its shape defined by the meandering Amtrak line, which makes up the northern boundary. Revitalization of areas to the south is already slowly filling the gaps to the thriving neighborhoods of Butchers Hill and Patterson Park. North of the Amtrak line, though, the scale of abandonment is truly breathtaking, notwithstanding small islands of re-investment around the former American Brewery or at the Dayspring transitional housing adaptive reuse of a former school. For the moment, though, the Amtrak line is a reasonable boundary even if once again a rail line will decide who is on "the right and the wrong sides of the tracks". The Hopkins biopark development is a gigantic experiment. At this point, its staggering investments allow only one direction: forward. No matter how the EBDI development turns out, with its massive relocation, it won't be a beacon of community-based planning.

Notes

1 The Baltimore Neighborhood Indicators Alliance-Jacob France Institute at the University of Baltimore (known as BNIA-JFI) is a non-profit organization whose core mission is to provide open access to meaningful, reliable, and actionable data about, and for, the City of Baltimore and its communities. http://bniajfi.org/about_bnia/

2 Joan Jacobsen, Vacants to Value, *The Abell Report*, Vol. 28, #5, Nov. 2015, pg. 6.

3 Baltimore City Department of Planning, *Green Network Plan*. http://planning.baltimorecity.gov/green-network-plan

4 Barry Yeoman, Left Behind in Sandtown, *CityLimits*, Jan. 1, 1998. http://citylimits.org/1998/01/01/left-behind-in-sandtown/

5 www.huduser.gov/portal/publications/affhsg/hope3.html

6 Timothy Wheeler, Habitat Group Rehabs 300th Home in Sandtown, *Baltimore Sun*, Dec. 11, 2011.

7 Luke Broadwater, Wells Fargo Agrees to Pay $175M Settlement in Pricing Discrimination Suit, *Baltimore Sun*, July 12, 2012.

8 Michael Rosenwald and Michael Fletcher, Why Couldn't $130 Million Transform One of Baltimore's Poorest Places?, *Washington Post*, May 2, 2015.

9 ACLU, *The Case of Thompson V. HUD: A Briefing on Segregation and Public Housing in Baltimore*, undated. www.aclu-md.org/uploaded_files/0000/0155/thompsonbriefing.pdf

10 Daniel P. Henson, Biography, *The Henson Development Company*. www.
hensondevelopmentco.com/index.cfm?page=about&section=bio
11 US Department of Housing and Urban Development, *Choice Neighborhoods*.
http://portal.hud.gov/hudportal/HUD?src=/program_offices/public_indian_
housing/programs/ph/cn
12 Mindy Thompson Fullilove, *Root Shock, How Tearing Up City Neighborhoods
Hurts America, and What We Can Do About It*, Random House, 2004. www.
newvillagepress.net/book/?GCOI=97660100655590
13 Nina Castells, *HOPE VI Neighborhood Spillover Effects in Baltimore*, HUD
Cityscape, Vol. 12, #1, 2010, pg. 65–98. www.jstor.org/stable/20868733?seq=1#
page_scan_tab_contents
14 ACLU, *The Case of Thompson V. HUD: A Briefing on Segregation and Public
Housing in Baltimore*, undated. www.aclu-md.org/uploaded_files/0000/0155/
thompsonbriefing.pdf
15 *Moving to Opportunity*, HUD 2016. http://portal.hud.gov/hudportal/HUD?src=/
programdescription/mto
16 Fenit Nirappil, *Washington Post*, Jan. 5, 2015.
17 Julia Day and Paul Graziano, Baltimore Housing summit at the Baltimore
Convention Center, Nov. 18–19, 2015. www.vacantstovalue.org/Content/Docs/
summit%20packet_final.pdf
18 Joan Jacobsen, Vacants to Value, *The Abell Report*, Vol. 28, #5, Nov. 2015.
www.abell.org/sites/default/files/files/cd-vacants2-value1115.pdf
19 *TRF Development Partners*. www.trfdevelopmentpartners.com/ourteam.html
20 Day and Graziano, Baltimore Housing summit.
21 Jeffery Gettleman, Ashes and Tears in the Lost Battle of Drug War, *New York
Times*, Oct. 18, 2002. www.nytimes.com/2002/10/18/us/ashes-and-tears-in-lost-
battle-of-drug-war.html
22 Author's notes taken at the event "Design Conversation #51, Baltimore, April 2,
2013.
23 Jack Shannon, Opening Remarks. Project documentation ArchPlan office
archive: A paper issued by East Baltimore Development Inc. titled "Master planning for phases II/III", Community Meeting, April 5, 2006.

2.4 Preservation, adaptive reuse and heritage

Preserving and recycling buildings is good for sustainability, good for economic development, provides authenticity and strengthens cultural heritage.

This old building is not good because it's old but it is old because it is good.
(Rodney Little, Maryland Historic Trust)

Some of my architecture seminars back in 1974 took place in what used to be the original headquarters of the Robert Bosch company in Stuttgart, Germany. My urban activism began with co-founding a group to save a medieval building from demolition. Three out of my first four architecture assignments in Baltimore were to design old buildings for new uses. Some of Baltimore's most creative architecture can be found in recycled buildings, which not only proves Rodney Little's favorite saying in the epigraph above, but shows that buildings can become even better with age.

Still, in a legacy city, the sheer number of abandoned and obsolete buildings from the industrial age can be a liability that is hard to turn into an asset, no matter how creative. Reuse of old buildings is an age-old practice. Adaptive reuse as a sustainability, economic development and revitalization argument is more recent. Preservation has come a long way from a focus on protecting architectural jewels and landmarks to caring about cultural heritage as a whole, mundane buildings included.

The preservationist Donavan Rypkema made the economic argument in his "Economics of Preservation"[1] as early as 1997. Preservation has since become an integral part of community development and sustainable community strategies on the state and federal level. In the current trend towards urban living, urbanity, place-making and authenticity have become necessary attributes. Nothing can deliver better on those points than historic buildings and settings that exemplify the various epochs of a city. Baltimore has many locally designated historic districts and enough structures that are listed in the National Register that it can compete with almost any other US city.[2] But the demolition and destruction of old buildings continues to be a threat to Baltimore and communities across the country. The Environmental

Protection Agency (EPA) calculated that building construction debris constitutes around a third of all waste generated in this country. EPA projected that over 27 per cent of existing buildings will be replaced between 2000 and 2030.[3]

The national trust challenge

Although there are plenty of success stories for adaptive reuse, obstacles prevent adaptive reuse from being the obvious "default" choice. Cost is one of them. Development in "green-fields" is cheaper than development in existing communities, and rehabilitation is often more expensive than new construction, even after the International Building Code was adjusted to allow flexibility for existing structures. As a result, there is still too much new development in the "green-fields" and, under the guise of "obsolescence", there is too much demolition in cities.

To get more developers to see old buildings as an asset instead of a demolition cost item is a national challenge. The National Trust for Historic Preservation (NTHP) set out to meet it together with the Urban Land Institute in the *Partnership for Building Reuse*.[4] Together, they studied successful adaptive reuse and the remaining obstacles in five cities across America. They just had to include Baltimore, a city with a very high percentage of historic buildings and a plethora of successful adaptive reuse projects.

Jim Lindberg, Planning Director at NTHP in Denver, is the leader of the partnership, and he introduced his team at a Baltimore kick-off meeting at Silo Point, which is a conversion of old grain silos into luxury condominiums in the Locust Point neighborhood. The community where immigrants once landed is located next to the National Park of Fort McHenry and is still surrounded by rail yards. Silo Point is a very creative and transformative example that even the most mundane industrial structures can be recycled.

Many may think of preservationists as past-oriented nostalgic people. With Michael Powe, the partnership has a PhD graduate with millennial credentials on the team, an energetic young man who is fluent in using GIS, someone who researches metrics such as cell phone usage, bars open after 10, "granularity" of building stock and "character score", all in the name of preservation. Michael talks about it in terms of older, smaller, better, economic development, livability metrics, being green and being cool, without ever mentioning architectural style or uttering the words *cornice*, or *pedestal*. With this refreshingly unorthodox approach to historic preservation, the Partnership for Reuse had no difficulty finding more than 90 locals from all walks of life who wanted to be partners and form volunteer working groups to scrutinize all the roadblocks standing in the way of building reuse.

Building codes, fire, and egress requirements and zoning are obstacles conspiring against reuse. Aside from larger cities having much stronger enforcement than outlying areas, in many instances, a rehabilitation project cannot neatly conform to rules that have clearly been developed for new development. The argument that existing roads, sewers and water lines would save money is often used by smart-growth advocates, but it does not always apply, especially where urban infrastructure is too deteriorated or feeble to support infill or reuse.

On the other hand, the adage that they "don't make 'em like this anymore" adds value and is responsible for one of the major findings of the research: A rich mix of structures, "diversity", as Michael Powe called it, pretty much guarantees that the assessed values of buildings are on average higher than in areas where urban renewal stratified the building age and destroyed neighborhood fabric and old structures.

Diversity of building age now has to be added to all the other diversity requirements that have become ingredients for successful communities, such as mixed-use, a modal mix in mobility offerings and demographic diversity in terms of age and ethnic background. In fact, Powe suggested that a mix of smaller, older structures results in more jobs, more local businesses – even more women or minority-owned businesses – and higher tax yields from additional density.[5]

This added value accrues slowly and over time, and could be the secret money fountain that makes adaptive reuse also work financially. As always, when greater investment is required up-front to create economic value in the long run, tools are needed to make those dollars available. Tax increment financing (TIF), tax credits or any number of other methods can generate up-front cash that is otherwise hard to come by.

Baltimore, with its record number of structures on the National Register of Historic Places, a listing that does not prevent demolition but is a prerequisite for obtaining preservation-based incentives, is well positioned to take advantage of incentives. With 72 per cent, Baltimore nationally also has the highest relative number of buildings built before 1945. If the team's findings are right, this isn't a liability but a gold mine for "granularity" and "character score", indices for how attractive a city is for immigrants, the creative class and millennials.[6] Baltimore's grit may just be the ticket that gets the city to the next level in a decades-long journey from an industrial center to a destination for knowledge and innovation. This whole new way of looking at preservation allows the surprise finding that the green effect from building reuse comes less from the embedded energy or saved materials and more from embedded character and authenticity. As the following examples show, Baltimore has been a trailblazer in reusing buildings and industrial sites for decades.

The battle for the preservation of the American Can Company

One of Baltimore's watershed preservation battles dates more than 30 years back. The story includes a villain, an engaged community and a savior and takes place in the setting of industrial decline accelerated by financial shenanigans.

The American Can Company had been closed, and its 2,000 employees were laid off as a result of a financial high-wire act that involved junk bonds, buy-out and liquidation of the nation's big can manufacturers.[7] The 10-acre American Can site sat across the street from the Anchorage redevelopment, Baltimore's first new residential waterfront development in working-class Canton.

Following the liquidation, developer Michael Swerdlow wanted to completely demolish the historic American Can complex to erect a dense mixed-use development, including a 22-story condo tower. The developer's Achilles heel was his intent to use federal funding from a City-managed UDAG community block grant. This brought up Section 106 of the National Historic Preservation Act of 1966, which forbids the destruction of historical assets in any project where federal funds are used.[8] A historic review determined that the Can Company was a historically contributing structure[9] and that the developer had not studied the option of adaptive reuse sufficiently.

Emboldened by the impasse on preservation, community activists collaborated with Baltimore's *Neighborhood Design Center* to produce a report about their own vision. It included demands for adaptive reuse and affordable housing. Understanding that this combination wasn't attainable without additional resources, the community insisted on the introduction of a council bill that would leverage *impact fees* on higher end waterfront projects to support affordable housing. The idea of leveraging luxury development for community benefits was then ahead of its time, but it resurfaced in recent *community benefits agreements* that are part of the Baltimore Horseshoe Casino, a recent expansion of the University of Maryland Biopark and the proposed Port Covington redevelopment.

The 1990 impact fee bill failed. Al Barry, then Assistant Director of Planning, explained that such a fee would "discourage development and force builders into the suburbs".[10] Swerdlow, indeed, gave up even without impact fee, abandoned his American National Plaza development and left for the Sunshine State, Florida.

The defeat of the demolition plan was the second victory for the community after defeating the freeways that would have traversed Canton and Fells Point.

The preservation of the American Can left the question of what to do with the buildings and their industrial heritage.

The young developer William Struever had already embraced preservation of industrial buildings in his Tindeco and Canton Cove projects

Figure 2.9 The American Can Company in 1987 when it stood vacant
© Library of Congress

without notable opposition, even though these were pivotal conversions of Baltimore's Canton waterfront. He purchased the American Can complex and developed a complex adaptive reuse project with a business incubator, company headquarters, a very cool restaurant in a former boiler room and a supermarket. The latter was a vestige from the Chertow plan, ending the area's longstanding status as a food desert. The Can Company redevelopment lifted the adaptive reuse of individual buildings to a new level by recycling an entire campus and creating a day-round destination. Struever repeated the campus approach at Clipper Mill in Woodberry, a modest community far away from the harbor, and in an even larger scale at the Procter and Gamble soap factory in Locust Point, a complex that should later become the headquarters of Under Armour.

Brownfield reuse

The community fire power was evoked again when Allied Signal began to dismantle its hulking plant prominently located in the Inner Harbor with a priceless view of downtown. The 21-acre chromium plant site was encapsulated as part of EPA brownfield clean-up.

Figure 2.10 The Allied Signal plant around 1978
© Brough Schamp photography

The Waterfront Coalition did not demand preservation, but neither did it foresee that anyone could build again on the hexavalent chromium saturated site sitting between historic Fells Point and the new Inner Harbor. The coalition wanted a 26-acre park, while the Honeywell Corporation, which had obtained the site from the defunct Allied Signal Company, had different ideas. With the help of a group of consultants (I was one of them), it showed that after the containment of the toxins, development was, indeed, possible. In 1992, after almost two years of wrangling, the community agreed to a Planned Unit Development (PUD) of 1.7 million square feet of mixed use with a maximum height of 180 feet and a 6-acre public use at the premium corner. The PUD was modified twice and allows now 2.8 million square feet of development and much taller buildings, such as the recently completed tower for energy giant Exelon.

The Allied site agreement was a pre-emptive move by the owners and potential developers for the time after an adjacent big brownfield right north of the Allied peninsula would have filled up, an area that was planned when the Allied Signal factory was still spewing smoke and chromium.

That area of what should become *Inner Harbor East* had been leveled for the urban expressway connections across the Inner Harbor that had been defeated. After the successful revitalization of the Inner Harbor and having leapfrogged all the way to Canton, Mayor Schaefer made his next waterfront move following the Planning Department's vision of a continuous promenade lined by new waterfront development. For the idea of a downtown extension to the east, he needed to avoid an uninspired single-story shopping center development proposed by developer and land owner Michael Silver. He did so by convincing Baltimore's "bread-man", the late John Paterakis, maker of all McDonalds rolls east of the Mississippi, to get the land from Silver, whom he had loaned some money anyway, and become a developer himself. To this day, the family-owned bakery runs its industrial baking operation on land that sits on the remaining land between Inner Harbor East and historic Fells Point.

Martin Millspaugh and Al Copp, who had overseen the Charles Center and Inner Harbor redevelopment as heads of quasi-governmental development corporations, engaged architect Stan Eckstut, who had just gained international status with his design for Battery Park, a much acclaimed urban waterfront redevelopment in Manhattan. Eckstut's award-winning Baltimore masterplan plan wrapped parking garages with mixed-use buildings, envisioned active shopping streets with wide sidewalks and up to 180-foot-tall buildings concentrated in the center with lower structures leaving open views around the peripheral promenade.

The City did the infrastructure, laying out a set of development lots along an urban cobblestone-paved street grid with a traffic circle, a monument, fixed bulkheads and retro lampposts. Unfortunately, in the cyclical world of real estate, the ready-to-build lots faced an economic slump. Baltimoreans at the time debated the wisdom of those public dollars that now sat there with no buildings in sight even though the area was declared an Empowerment Zone. They reneged on a promise to buy the land back from Paterakis.

When Kurt Schmoke, an Ivy League graduate and successful attorney, became the first elected African American Mayor of Baltimore, he was brimming with ideas such as the renewal of Sandtown Winchester, legalization of drugs and a new Eco Industrial Park for the Baltimore brownfields of Fairfield. In 1996, Schmoke landed a coup that reverberated around the country and was worth a national article by noted syndicated columnist Neil Peirce: Sylvan Learning Centers, a tutoring and testing services company, relocated from leafy suburban Howard County to Baltimore's Inner Harbor East and became one of the first corporations to revert the decades old trend in the other direction. At the time Douglas Becker, head of Sylvan, was Baltimore's number one entrepreneurial wunderkind. At 28 years old and a recent graduate from Baltimore's Gilman school, Becker was already a millionaire profiled in the *Fortune Magazine*.[11] Peirce wrote at the time:

> The decision of Sylvan Learning Systems to move its world headquarters to the Baltimore waterfront is the kind of development the Clinton administration dreamed of when it proposed empowerment zones for America's cities. . . .
>
> It's the first major corporation to move to central Baltimore in more than 20 years and eventually will employ 600. 'There's real excitement for our employees and customers in a downtown location,' [Becker] told me. 'You have to come to the city for first-rate amenities, culture, the heart of commerce – things you're hard-pressed to find in the suburbs'.[12]

My involvement in the matter began when Paterakis and Mayor Kurt Schmoke followed Doug Becker's Sylvan coup with a second one they thought was even bolder: a 450-foot-high hotel right at the water's edge

Figure 2.11 A simulation of the originally intended height for the planned Harbor East hotel

that both envisioned as a convention center hotel, in spite of the significant distance to the actual convention center.

I saw the problem as one of urban design: The tall hotel would not only shatter the maximum height limits established by Eckstut's plan, but would also be positioned at the edge where the plan mandated low buildings. The AIA Urban Design Committee launched photo montages showing the tall hotel across the water and eventually succeeded in lowering the height of the hotel to 225 feet, still far above the masterplan limits. The hotel deal was greased by tax exemption for 25 years.

The hotel really broke the ice, and investors started to flood in. A Whole Foods store was placed to bring people to the site. Today the entire new quarter is complete and exhibits a newness that is detested by the same people who also consider the Inner Harbor as inauthentic. The arguments on whether the baker got too much of a break on taxes, whether Harbor East sapped energy out of the historic downtown and if Baltimore really accrued any benefit from having developed that part of town continue to this day. Harbor East is used by friends and foes as a foil to the current debate about *Port Covington*, with 250 acres to be the largest brownfield redevelopment yet.

The highlights of Baltimore's waterfront battles are preservation of industrial heritage, saving working-class communities from gentrification, community benefits, gauging the breaking point for a developer to be spooked and transportation and gridlock, in short, the topics of public debate in almost any legacy city. Meanwhile, the reuse of industrial buildings created some of the most identifiable authentic Baltimore buildings, while new construction on large industrial brownfield sites produced Baltimore's more generic places, free of grit or references to the industrial past but on par with the amenities of the competing sunbelt cities. The iconic Domino Sugar sign still beckons across the harbor, indicating one of the few still functional production sites.

Class B offices to apartments

Adaptive reuse is not limited to the conversion of former industrial buildings to lofts or offices. Obsolete class B or even C office buildings can become downtown apartments, another strong trend across America.

In Baltimore's "financial district" with its narrower streets, typical for a legacy city, smaller historic office buildings often lack daylight and views. When I told an investor who had happily bought an obsolete office building with a burger shop at the bottom that I couldn't be his conversion architect because there wasn't enough daylight for attractive apartments, he didn't understand why I cared. He just saw a hot market. Some taller and bigger office buildings, though, have become fantastic conversions and have contributed to downtown being Baltimore's fastest-growing neighborhood.

The biggest such conversion is the former Maryland National Bank, a 34-story-high rise that is as idiosyncratic to Baltimore's skyline as is the "Empire State Building" to New York's. It now houses 447 apartments, and many still need to be filled. The Munsey Building, Baltimore's first major downtown conversion, struggled to fill its apartments in 2002, and the massive conversion of the former Baltimore Gas and Electric headquarters into apartments is a big money loser, according to David Hillman, the owner of Southern Management, which has also converted the former downtown Hechts department store into the Atrium Apartments and a former Standard Oil and then government office building into The Standard.[13] The problem stems from the high cost of conversion that cannot easily be balanced by equally high rents in districts that are either still marred by vacancy or lack amenities such a green spaces or dog parks.

The complaints of developers about losing money[14] led the Mayor and City Council to enact tax credits for apartments in downtown and select target areas. A 15-year property tax incentive bill[15] grants 100 per cent tax relief for years 1 and 2, then diminishes the credit from 80 per cent to 20 per cent from years 3 through 15, provided a project has at least 50 apartments and is LEED silver or better. Combined with Empowerment Zone tax credits or historic tax credits, there may be no property taxes way beyond the first two years.

The City tax credit cannot make up for the fact that the Maryland State historic tax credit budget, with now only $7 million annually, is a mere shadow of what it once was and way too small to match the high demand.

As long as local, regional and statewide planning allows easy access to new development areas outside cities, towns and villages, adaptive reuse will remain the more expensive option. The long-term or environmental costs of sprawl[16] aren't accounted for in a developer's proforma. It makes sense, then, that the State would offset some of the developer's cost because it can avoid the cost of dispersed transportation, utility and infrastructure networks and get the benefit of attracting a qualified, young and dynamic workforce that wants to live urban, a key to the revitalization of the legacy city.

Notes

1 Donavan Rypkema, *The Economics of Historic Preservation: A Community Leader's Guide*, The National Trust for Historic Preservation, 1994.
2 Time Magazine, *These Are America's Best Cities for Historic Sites*, July 22, 2015. http://time.com/3961200/america-best-cities-historic-sites/

3 Sustainable Management of Construction and Demolition Materials, *EPA*. www.epa.gov/smm/sustainable-management-construction-and-demolition-materials

4 National Trust for Historic Preservation, Urban Land Institute, *National Partnership for Building Reuse*, 2012. Launched in Los Angeles, the five cities of Detroit Chicago, Philadelphia, Baltimore and Los Angeles participated in the initiative culminating in a national publication planned for 2016. http://forum.savingplaces.org/act/pgl/pbr

5 Preservation Green Lab, *Older, Smaller, Better, Measuring How the Character of Buildings and Blocks Influences Urban Vitality*, May 2014. http://forum.savingplaces.org/HigherLogic/System/DownloadDocument File.ashx?DocumentFileKey=b73e8fc7-7fb2-0fc7-202c-d0ed58ff3089&force Dialog=0

6 Preservation Green Lab, *Building on Baltimore's History*, The Partnership for Building Reuse, Nov. 2014. http://forum.savingplaces.org/HigherLogic/System/ DownloadDocumentFile.ashx?DocumentFileKey=439898f5-c580-757c-e9fd-d636088a31e0&forceDialog=0

7 Sherry Olson, *The Building of an American City*, Johns Hopkins University Press, 1997 pg. 393.

8 Leslie Barras, *Section 106 of the National Historic Preservation Act*, National Trust for Historic Preservation, 2010.

9 Historic American Engineering Record Mid-Atlantic Region, National Park Service Department of the Interior Philadelphia, PA, *American Can Company: Boston & Hudson Streets Baltimore City, HAER NO. MD-68*, 1988. http://cdn.loc.gov/master/pnp/habshaer/md/md1100/md1146/data/md1146data.pdf

10 *Baltimore Sun*, Nov. 2, 1990. Quoted via Andy Merrifield, "Dialectical Urbanism: Social struggles in the capitalistic city", *Monthly Review Press*, 2002.

11 Alison Rogers, With a Little Help From Their Friends, *Fortune Magazine*, Sept. 19, 1994. http://archive.fortune.com/magazines/fortune/fortune_archive/1994/09/19/79735/index.htm

12 Neil Peirce, Enterprise Zone Lures Business Back to City Baltimore's Coup Bodes Well For Clinton's Urban Revitalization Plan, *The Philadelphia Inquirer*, Feb. 26, 1997.

13 James Briggs, Apartment Conversions Too Costly for Baltimore Developers, *Baltimore Business Journal*, Mar. 9, 2012. http://wpmllc.com/pdf/BBJ_Article.pdf

14 Ibid.

15 Ivonne Wenger, City Council Approvals Tax Breaks to Spur Baltimore Development, *Baltimore Sun*, June 23, 2014. http://articles.baltimoresun.com/2014-06-23/news/bs-md-ci-tax-credits-development-20140623_1_tax-bills-tax-breaks-property-tax

16 Northeast-Midwest Institute, The Environmental and Energy Conservation Benefits of the Maryland Historic Tax Credit Program, *Abell Report* 2008. www.preservationnation.org/information-center/economics-of-revitalization/rehabilitation-tax-credits/additional-resources/EnvEnergyImpactsMDHistTaxCredit.pdf

2.5 Innovation and making

The making of things is not obsolete. Innovation and creativity can empower people and create new jobs. Picking up on some traditional human-centered production can connect people to history, the land and a city's culture.

How did the Baltimore metro area become one of only 19 global cities named *Knowledge Capitals*?[1] What gives Baltimore the appeal to be voted one of the top cities in the nation for millennial college students?[2] To what extent can the renaissance of making, innovation or good old manufacturing break the cycles of joblessness and poverty? Does the knowledge economy offer opportunities to break out of the cycles of poverty or does it just further reinforce them?

The story of the creative vibes in Baltimore cannot be told without the Maryland Institute College of Art (MICA), the Station North Arts and Entertainment District (SNAED) and the role that the influx of students has played in the revitalization of an area that had been written off as dead a mere dozen years ago and has celebrated a comeback as a center of creativity and art. Station North is one of the first State-designated arts and entertainment districts in the country. Neither can it be understood without factoring in the industrial heritage, the reinvention of new industries in old spaces and Baltimore's culture of making stuff. Many would argue that all of the above would not have happened without a vibrant and somewhat stealth underground arts and music scene.

The feverish pace of start-up pitch events taking place across the country and the construction of maker spaces, incubators, angel funders and innovation districts may strike many as a fad. But it could be the chance to finally lift those that have been left behind for so long. Recycling industrial wasteland may take care of the geographical inelasticity problem but still leaves behind the people that remain in disadvantaged communities, unemployed and stuck in concentrations of poverty.

Many initiatives such as Baltimore Corps or Innovation Village[3] are trying to close this wide gap between the skills that are needed and the skills people have.

Finding a way to distribute these seeds of creativity and innovation more equitably, and to a much broader section of the populace for wealth creation and self-support, would make the renaissance of this *inelastic* formerly industrial city truly complete. The stories that follow show attempts to do just that.

The Maryland College of Art

Baltimore's famed anchor institutions from Johns Hopkins University to Maryland College of Art (MICA) may have come late to the understanding that their fate is tied to that of their hometown. But once that insight was there, these stakeholders stepped up and created new paradigms.

Although my notes from that meeting are long gone, I vividly recall a meeting with then–MICA President Fred Lazarus some 25 years back for which I had asked to market my young architecture firm. By then, Lazarus had been President of MICA for about 15 years. His goals for his Art Institute were incredibly clear and at the time seemed utterly unattainable. He wanted to double enrollment and become one of the top art schools in the country – I believe he aimed for the number two spot. Our meeting took place in MICA's flagship building, the beautiful Italianesque Renaissance headquarter constructed in 1905 with funds from philanthropist Andrew Carnegie as a replacement of the Center Market building that had been destroyed by Baltimore's big fire in 1904.[4]

Lazarus explained to me how MICA understands that it needs to engage with the communities around it and with other anchor institutions as well. By the time Lazarus retired in 2014, he had delivered on all his goals: Enrollment has doubled, the school is ranked in the top 10 graduate programs,[5] the campus has grown exponentially, and the school has added a program for social design and created a presence on the heavily disinvested North Avenue corridor and Baltimore's ravaged Middle East neighborhood through filling abandoned industrial buildings and one clerical facility. The school has shifted the architectural standards with its asymmetrical fully glass-clad Brown Center, a programmatic compendium to the 1905 headquarters building. MICA partners with Johns Hopkins University in a dual-degree program[6] that teaches design thinking and business thinking, is engaged with Baltimore's Central Partnership to achieve revitalization of a dozen or so communities and lately supports the West Baltimore Innovation Village.

Art as neighborhood regenerator

Station North is more than the well-worn story of artists as urban pioneers that began in Manhattan's SoHo some 40 years ago as a watershed moment in how urban regeneration was viewed. Back then, government still tried to stifle the burgeoning artists and their shops and galleries with zoning restrictions and code violation notices. In version 2.0 of "urban regeneration through art", government plays a supportive role. For example, Station North is a State-designated A&E district that aims to protect artists from gentrification by providing tax credits to artists.[7] State and local government are seeing arts districts as major revitalization incubators. There are three such districts in Baltimore, and Station North is probably the most diverse one owing to the fact that it originated in a quite distressed area. The story of Station North has many mothers and fathers and is told in different ways, depending on whom one asks.

Some artists were here long before it became a designated district. But they were penned up in the maze of the former Crown, Cork and Seal bottle-capping company complex, a truly amazing adaptive reuse in its own right.

Early evidence of art in Station North were also the Everyman Theater and the Charles movie theater that had opened in a trolley bus barn. Both served a certain stratum of the regional population and sparked a couple of restaurants, but remained isolated for a long time. Although these early art roots were key in getting the A&E district approved, they alone couldn't leverage the revitalization of the surrounding community until they joined hands with neighbors to achieve things together. Initially they met each other only at chance encounters to discuss the rare pioneering new development, such as the 32 contemporary townhomes that my architecture firm designed on a vacant lot equidistant from the train station and the artists' complex. All this is different now.

Partnerships began to play a vital role. They include private developers, non-profits, institutions, freelancers, local government and various community organizations that overlap with the district. The "arts district" provides the glue that bonds together neighborhoods across what were formerly distinct boundaries. It is understood that residents lived there before the artists came and want to continue to live there. It is understood that all residents share an interest in good services.

These complexities take shape in a variety of organizational forms. There is the collaboration between three educational powerhouses: the Maryland Institute College of Art (MICA), the University of Baltimore (UB) and Johns Hopkins University (JHU), based on their 2008 assessment that the quite disinvested sector of "central Baltimore" (the area between Penn Station and Hopkins) presented a challenge for all three universities and for their long-term well-being. It brought about the Central Baltimore Higher Education Collaborative. From it flowed the Central Baltimore Partnership (CBP). The arts and entertainment district itself is organized by the non-profit Station North Arts & Entertainment, Inc. Together these organizations represent the diversity of interests that are necessary to revitalize a community beyond one dimension into a place where *live* and *work* are at least as important as *learn* and *play*. Instead of each organization playing in its respective corner – the one doing the housing, the other the teaching and the third the arts – these strands are now intertwined in creative ways to transform large area in a sustainable and equitable way.

Jubilee Baltimore's "City Arts Building", which provided affordable housing for artists in newly constructed studio type, was an important seed that quickly filled in spite of its location at the periphery of the arts district at the corner of Oliver and Greenmount, once "the corner of life and death", how developer Charlie Duff[8] put it (a double entendre referring also to one of Baltimore's oldest cemeteries across the street). Jubilee and its partners also grabbed the adjacent lot on Oliver Street, put modern townhomes on it and renovated another dozen historic rowhouses until the street was free of boarded houses and vacant lots. Now 400 artists live and work on this street alone.

Next to those developments, the former Lebow industrial building has been transformed into the public Baltimore Design School, the city's first all new middle and high school in many years. The project was creatively developed by a private development entity and then leased back by the Baltimore City school system. Historic tax credits were part of its complicated funding scheme.

A creative partnership was also needed to take on the long vacant Centre Theater project. In an auction by a team that also included Jubilee Baltimore, MICA bought for little more than one dollar per square foot, this Art Deco structure that has become *The Impact Hub* and home to several non-profits and start-ups. The nearby historic Parkway Theater, also on North Avenue, is currently under construction to become the home of the *Baltimore Film Festival*. A low-key art-friendly developer has assembled a host of tenants in the sprawling old North Avenue Market, long shuttered and now the home for *The Wind Up Space*, a mixed gallery and event space, an Irish Pub, a print shop and an employee-owned bookstore/cafe. Even the temporary loss of one of the first art hub venues, *The Load of Fun*, closed due to code issues, was painful, but the complex reopened as *The Motor House*, with a theater, non-profits and incubator office spaces, all funded by the local Deutsch Foundation dedicated to supporting the arts.

This slew of arts-themed development allowed Amtrak to advertise a request for qualifications for a master developer for a set of development lots located at Baltimore's main train station. This shows that, embedded in partnerships, the arts, indeed, can regenerate a neighborhood.

The CBP meanwhile reports significant progress as well.

The Homewood Community Partners Initiative, a Call to Action: Findings and Recommendations[9] laid out a 10-year action plan that includes a very specific inventory and a clear set of goals, such as adding 3,000 new households to the area, eliminating all vacant houses and vacant lots while preserving and adding affordable housing and racial and economic diversity. The strategy has an estimated price tag of $17.5 million for gap financing alone.

"In 10 years, no matter where you are within these 10 neighborhoods, you will be glad you are there", said Charlie Duff, a board member of the CBP, of the desired outcome, adding that folks saw the value of their homes stabilized and new services come to the area.[10] This may sound similar to many other plans in Baltimore, but what makes it different is that at the three-year mark, Duff reported astounding results: 265 houses had been rehabbed, 500 new housing units were constructed or are currently under construction and every one of the 10 communities in the partnership has seen a share of improvement. One hundred and fifty-one units are designated as affordable.

If all goes well, old-time residents will remain in place, newcomers will continue to renovate individual homes and the neighborhood will remain "Baltimore quirky" instead of becoming "Washington gentrified".

Maker spaces

Open Works[11] is a non-profit that provides access to tools and technology and knowledge. It is designed to spur creativity and combine it with entrepreneurial spirit in a place that doesn't break the bank. Open Works is

Figure 2.12 The Open Works maker-space in the old Railway Express facility
© The author

located at the eastern edge of the Station North arts district and is also part of the Greenmount West revitalization, an attempt to turn around a very disinvested corridor. It was developed by the non-profit Baltimore Arts Realty Corporation (BARCO), which was founded with the specific purpose of developing a space such as Open Works.

BARCO explains on its website that their "focus is on the acquisition, development, leasing, and management of properties in Baltimore's three Arts and Entertainment Districts that enable creative individuals, small businesses and organizations to work and thrive". BARCO in turn is a subsidiary of the local Deutsch Foundation. Will Holman, a trained architect, is the general manager of Open Works and instrumental in getting the 34,000-square-foot facility rehabilitated and ready to go in just 12 months. According to the *Baltimore Business Journal*, Open Works is the 6th largest maker space in the country.[12] At Open Works opening ceremony, the Mayor, the Congressman, a State Delegate and the head of the Baltimore Development Corporation talked about how important it is to have a comprehensive view of jobs, art, education, community development and social justice.

Open Works occupies the massive 1920 two-story structure, former Baltimore Railway Express operation near Baltimore's Penn Station, a conversion that cost about $5 million for construction alone. The program has everything from a café occupying a visible streetcorner with view of the historic Greenmount Cemetery to space for job training and workforce development, rental work spaces, workshops for textile, digital media, 3-D printing, wood metal, C&C machines and a computer lab. "We will not train and pray", Holman tells me, but cater to actual employment needs of the kind the local Abell Foundation recently identified in its "Best Prospects" report[13] for jobs without a college degree. (Abell also supported the maker-space project.)

Holman explains that Open Works is a three-legged stool supported by education, membership and rental space. Even though the project sits around the corner from *Area 405*, an artists' cooperative and event space, and the *Station North Tool Library*, both small-scale adaptations of the art and maker culture, there is friendly partnership among all three. "This isn't a situation where we share all one cake", Holman says, "we all want to grow together". He cites a statistic that says that Baltimore had an increase of 67 per cent in small scale manufacturing with one to five employees since 2003, a number that the Baltimore Development Corporation derived from census information. In Holman's mind, this is a clear indicator that Baltimore can grow a manufacturing base again.

Holman's research of maker spaces has found 318 such operations in the United States; most are part time and member driven, some institution based, some for-profit and some not. Two facilities he mentioned as good precedents for his Baltimore project are the 40,000-square-foot Artisans Asylum in Somerville, MA, and the Columbus, OH–based Idea Foundry.

Holman suggested the YMCA as an organizational model; like the Y, he points out, resources are pooled in a non-profit setting, the facilities are supported by members and they are open to the public.

Maker spaces are no substitute for an industrial base of a local or national economy, but they are seeds that provide a service that leverages people skills through training. The assumption is that there will be discovery and development of goods and products that lend themselves to the type of decentralized production that can be provided by the new sharing economy and the entrepreneurs who embrace it.

The next example of this thinking is corporate in nature.

Under Armour

The fame of many cities is closely tied to their famous home industries. Detroit, of course, rose and fell with Ford, General Motors and Chrysler. Pittsburgh can't be thought of without US Steel, the glass giant PPG or the Heinz Ketchup Empire. Baltimore is a bit different: Its core industries were the railroads, steel, shipbuilding and the port, but it wasn't a company town in which one or two companies pulled all the strings. Even though Bethlehem Steel, the largest employer, certainly had aspired to the concept of a company town in which workers would be beholden to the company for work, housing, purchases and entertainment, Baltimore then was a very large city and had too many other big players for any one of them to become its signature imprint. Today, Baltimore isn't home to a single Fortune 500 company. Pittsburgh, by comparison, has six.[14] But there is a Baltimore company growing rapidly and seeking to shape its hometown: Under Armour (UA). The sports apparel underdog that set out to conquer not only Puma and Adidas, but also brand leader and giant Nike, is set to leave its mark on manufacturing and on the City of Baltimore itself.

Under Armour has bought 260 acres of industrial land on Baltimore's "second waterfront", the Middle Branch, which is separated from the famous Inner Harbor by a large peninsula called South Baltimore. UA not only wants to build a new global headquarters, but to surround it with a small city of its own, which would become the largest urban renewal project in the history of Baltimore, even bigger than the redevelopment of downtown at the Inner Harbor. Busting out of its current Harbor-facing headquarters, UA has already relocated a small part of its operations in Port Covington by moving into the big box of a failed Sam's Club and remodeling a large former bus garage.

Port Covington and Westport had been part of the heart of a manufacturing-based economy when Baltimore was a place of innovation. Port Covington boasted the most efficient conveyor of coal from rail trucks to ships and presented the port's access to inland markets. The UA project briefly split the city into those who supported it and the use of a record size of tax increment financing to fund infrastructure and those who opposed it on the grounds that a wealthy company would need any "subsidies". After a few months of vigorous debates and oversized city council hearings on TIF bonds, the matter was settled with an unprecedented community benefits agreement negotiated directly with neighboring communities and representatives of a church coalition that represents disadvantaged communities across the city. In the context of manufacturing and innovation, one aspect of Under Armour's development is particularly interesting: local production.

UA's "Lighthouse" facility currently accommodated in the old bus garage (*City Garage*) is nothing less than a revolutionary new approach to manufacturing. It has the potential of completely re-shaping how production has been done for more than half a century, most recently offshore. That is where Under Armour's products are made today as well. But UA owner Kevin Plank sees the writing on the wall: labor cost that rises in low-wage countries, automation and robots reducing labor's share in production, and an increasing demand for localized customization of specialized high-quality goods. All that make offshore production less and less advantageous.

Lighthouse is approaching these emerging trends regarding labor cost from several sides: first by trying to reduce the amount of manual labor for their shoes by reducing the currently needed 50 or so parts with a shoe made from just a handful of components. The other innovation involves the reversal of a standard staple of the industrial economy: the economy of scale. Instead of having these new shoes made in a giant factory with a very high output of identical products to be shipped all around the world, Plank is envisioning small and highly flexible production units that can serve local markets with products that are custom tailored to local conditions.

Lighthouse is Plank's prototype and operates in City Garage in Baltimore.

It is a boutique style operation in one part of City Garage, a multi-use hub of innovation, UA's version of factory, incubator, training facility and maker space all under one roof.

This type of "Starbucksing of production"[15] will never employ thousands of Baltimoreans. That would be counter to the concept. But if this model of production works out here and in many other places where it currently is being tested, not only will it make production local again, but also it can be applied to many other products. Overall, it could have tremendous impact on the local labor market, with City Garage becoming a laboratory for the conversion of a "rustbelt city" to a "brainbelt city".

Robots

The Uber driver was a cabby before and knew how to turn left on Broening Highway, an industrial thoroughfare serving the Seagirt Terminal of the Port and named after a former mayor of Baltimore, even though Google told him right. We passed the brand new Amazon 1-million-square-foot "fulfillment center" where more than 3,000 people and countless robots operate one of the brick-and-mortar manifestations of online shopping. My destination is another spanking new industrial building: a 200,000-square-foot space for actually making stuff, although its output will become even more automated. Fully operational as of Fall 2016, Blueprint Robotics employs 125 people, but only 57 work on the factory floor where they can produce enough residential wall and floor panels per year to cover the entire 1-million-square-foot floor area of the gigantic nearby Amazon Center. That's a lot of homes. Seventy per cent of all homes are done by homebuilders that do only 5 to 50 homes per year. The promise of wall panels assembled in the factory is higher precision and a much shorter construction period. The downside is that parts need to be transported and then still need to be assembled in the field.

CEO Jerome Smalley calls his new Baltimore firm a "proof of concept plant".[16] A big investor backs him, trusting that Smalley is up to a promising future. The Baltimore model is supposed to eventually march across the United States, the ideal market area for each plant would be 250 miles. The initial plant will cover a market from Richmond to Boston.

Smalley points to a few gleaming tractor trailers lined up in the expansive yard. Even though the fleet dons the factory logo and colors, transportation will be outsourced to a logistics company. I observe robots doing astonishing tricks of routing and cutting wood inside sealed boxes into which the lumber is pulled for "treatment" as needed. A computer screen is the only worker–machine interface. A German-speaking crew passes by, the best paid workers in sight, doing the initial installation and calibration of the Weinmann carpentry machines. The robotic machines are all imported from a small town near Stuttgart, Germany. The pay at Blueprint Robotics isn't bad either; no minimum wage there: The starting wage, according to Jerome Smalley, will be $20. That is more than Amazon pays where humans are less the operators of the robots but their peers are in danger of being replaced by robots that find and package the correct product in the correct box for the right consumer in a fully automated process. Such a fully automated future isn't in sight for Blueprint Robotics, where the complicated machines need to be reprogrammed for each custom-designed house.

Somewhere between the giant cranes of the Port where Baltimore, the Domino Sugar factory, Amazon, and the robotic production of homes lies Baltimore's industrial future.

Brownfield redevelopment

The future of Sparrows Point, first as a steel-making location and then just as a location, has been debated for decades. For a long time, it was a sacrilege to think beyond the steel mill that was once the pride of the region and whose final 2,600 workers still mostly lived in the area. Additionally, Baltimore County's Department of Economic Development was focused on assisting the now-unemployed former employees to transition into a world after Sparrows Point, while still fueling the small flame of hope that a savior would appear to rescue the plant and fire up the furnaces again. Without much fanfare, the Baltimore County Executive convened a group of private business representatives to think about how some industrial production and a Port of Baltimore expansion could co-exist.

While steel workers were still trying to find a new steel mill buyer, the local City Paper broke the taboo and invited area architects and planners to imagine a different future and to think big about the Sparrows Point peninsula.[17]

My firm was one of those being asked to create "a vision" and, preferably, eye-catching images. (Architects are always asked to draw "pretty pictures".) Yet, I did not want to fall into this trap. One of the other firms, known for so-called life-style architecture, did show less hesitation and proposed a gigantic Coney Island style amusement park.

Instead of wracking my brain for "the big idea", I tried to get a sense of the land down there at the southern tip of the Baltimore Beltway where Key Bridge crosses the Chesapeake and allows a fantastic view from up high across Sparrows Point.

The area is more than 3,400 acres large. Laid over top of downtown, Sparrows Point would cover the entire area of downtown Baltimore from the Inner Harbor to North Avenue and from Martin Luther King Boulevard in the west to Caroline Street in the east. An area this large needs more than just one idea; it needs a gradual transformation and thousands of individuals to provide ideas and expertise. Not to mention gigantic amounts of capital to invest.

Still, without a plan that casts far into the future, one would never get anything but individual projects of opportunity. Sparrows Point is really a place where the much overused *vision* is needed.

Thinking about where else in the world large amounts of derelict industrial waterfront property were successfully converted, the London Docklands came to mind. While working as an intern at the Greater London Council (GLC) in the mid-1970s, I had seen the many plans that had been prepared for London's vast obsolete port areas. Labor's fiery "Red Ken" Livingstone then chaired the GLC (he would later become Mayor) and was one who realized the potential of obsolete industrial land on the waterfront right along with Baltimore's Mayor William Donald Schaefer.

But the conservative free market Prime Minister Margret Thatcher dissolved the GLC and "released" the Docklands from the world of planners to the world of developers and profit. A wild but short-lived building boom resulted in the spectacular financial bust of Canary Wharf. Eventually Canary Wharf recovered, and the Docklands became a serious part of London with transit, jobs, housing and entertainment and many examples of innovative architecture and good and bad urban design. In contrast to Sparrows Point, though, the Docklands are almost contiguous with downtown London. So are other examples of port reclamation sites, such as HafenCity, Hamburg, and the Kop van Zuid area in Rotterdam. These precedents show that a compromise between big plans and a pragmatic approach is needed even for places that can act as extensions of center cities. Reclamation efforts could be similar to those in the former German rustbelt of the "Ruhrgebiet" or, closer by, New York's Freshkills, a 2,200-acre transformation from garbage landfill to urban park.[18]

To bring more central locations into play, the State-run Port Authority could trade their currently disjointed locations inside the city for a more consolidated operation on Sparrows Point – a stretch, for sure, given how rare truly regional planning is in Baltimore, especially when it comes to swapping assets. The areas freed by a consolidated port could be extremely valuable in truly large picture thinking about the future of Sparrows Point.

Baltimore County did think big when it created the new town concepts for Owings Mills and White Marsh in an great effort to protect the rural north county – as big as Prince George's County, when it developed National Harbor, a new development just as far from downtown Washington as Sparrows Point is from Baltimore, although much smaller than the steel brownfield.

In a region that is projected to grow by another 600,000 residents by 2030, developing large tracts of land at the desirable water's edge with good access and infrastructure as more than a mono-culture of distribution warehouses is not at all unreasonable, serious contamination notwithstanding. Whether

Sparrows Point, Locust Point or Dundalk, any of these places would be eminently more reasonable for growth than additional sprawl into the rural areas. Couldn't some 40,000–50,000 people live in a new town on Sparrows Point? And couldn't that still leave large tracts of land for parks and recreation and industrial production with rail and deep-water access? Maybe there would even be a bit of space left for an amusement park, as there once was one at the end of a trolley line at North Point Park on Millers Island.

The time to think about the long-term future of Sparrows Point is now, but the big picture approach is the route not yet taken. The 300,000 square feet of FedEx Ground distribution warehouse, an announced Harley David-son Riding Academy training center, and the announcement of a 150-acre shopping center are maybe impressive as an indication that businesses are interested in the huge brownfield now called *Tradepoint Atlantic*.

The spokesperson for the organization with the same name overseeing the redevelopment was gushing about the shopping center: "It's going to be at our front door. . . . we will have 10,000 to 15,000 jobs here at the end of the build-out in about 10 years and this will be a place for amenities for our tenants' employees".[19]

As if America and Baltimore County weren't one of the most "over-retailed" spaces on the planet in terms of square feet of available retail per resident (the United States has over 46 square feet for each resident, the United Kingdom 23 and Canada 13). Gushing about new fast food places, a hotel, a grocery store and a gas station as the front door of a 3,100-acre site indicates far too much modesty. People might say one has to start somewhere, but what is the big idea? What is the long-range plan? What, in the end, should Sparrows Point become for the region? The latest announcement, that Baltimore's Under Armour was placing a 1-million-square-foot distribution center on the peninsula, could just be another incremental step. It could, however, also be the beginning of a much larger interplay between one of the largest brownfields on the East Coast and one of the most ambitious corporations in America, now with one foot in the city and one in the county.

The incredible power of open-source 3-D product makers

The conference titled "Prosthetists Meet Printers", organized by the *e-NABLE* group, took place on a bright fall morning at the venerable Johns Hopkins Hospital in Baltimore. To the surprise of the organizers, more than 400 people filled the auditorium at this first-time gathering.

What brought me to the conference was my grandson, who is a wearer of a prosthetic hand. He and his father customized the online hand 3-D printed designs as early adopters of the technology. As a founding member of e-NABLE, father and son also became the creators of the *Ody* and *Talon* hands. The event proved important beyond this personal tie.

The conference upended in a most revolutionary way the traditional set-up of health care where doctors prescribe expensive items made by a powerful industrial complex to patients who often can't afford them or have to wait way too long to get them. At this conference, patients, doctors, prosthetic experts and layperson makers all sat in one space, and perhaps for the first time in modern history, patients were empowered to become the makers.

In 1861, in a move reminiscent of the new movement, founder James Edward Hanger fixed his own amputated leg up with a prosthesis made from barrel staves. Hanger went on to become one of the most recognized manufacturers of prosthetic devices. The company was a conference sponsor. Their support of a potentially threatening innovation train was indicative of the mash-up of old and new paradigms that characterized the entire conference. In the halls of Hopkins– which are usually reserved to professional elites – kids, parents, grandparents, professors, wearers of prosthetics, doctors, kinesthesiologists and the 3-D printer makers mingled and convened as a diverse, colorful and restless audience.

New tools made this gathering possible: open-source data sharing, 3-D printing, tool sharing and crowd-sourced manufacturing. In just a couple of years, crowd-sourced making brought about prosthetic refinements that matched or even surpassed devices for which the established industry had needed decades of research and product development, approval processes and regulatory hoop jumping.

Unknown to many, congenital conditions or bleeding in certain early phases of pregnancy cause hundreds of thousands of children to be born with smaller or larger deficiencies in their extremities, especially hands. Add to this the victims of injuries from war caused by explosive devices and accidents, and one sees a significant need for artificial limbs. The e-NABLE network matches, especially, children in need of prosthetic limbs with those who can make them with 3-D printers.

It has become fashionable to call upheavals of this kind "disruptive inno-vations". Hanger Prosthetics and Johns Hopkins Professor *Albert Chi*, a trauma surgeon and Reserve Lieutenant of the US Navy, embraced the new bottom-up competition and responded smarter than the taxi lobby, which is engaged in a futile fight with disrupter Uber. Professor Chi has been in contact with the e-NABLERs for some time and has even adopted the 3-D printing method for some products in his own group. In organizing and hosting this maker conference, he bridged the cutting-edge research world of Hopkins, where he collaborates with the Applied Physics Lab (APL) and works on "myoelectric" artificial limbs that can be controlled by the mind, with the power of the people who use prosthetics. The homemade prosthetic devices that were on display in at Hopkins' developed a new esthetic as well. Emulating the most popular colorful action figures, the bulk and crudeness, which are still hallmarks of much of additive plastic printing, were turned into an asset. Instead of feeling disadvantaged, the kids felt empowered by these hands and arms that didn't even try to look natural.

Manual labor

Not all trends point towards a reduction of labor in the process of making; some go in the other direction. Local craft has become increasingly a marketable brand, from craft beers to pottery and locally grown organic foods. Those counter-movements are driven by concerns for health and a desire for authenticity, durability and value in a world of sameness and cheap mass production.

The two Baltimore examples of *deconstruction* and urban farming take those desires and connect them to re-entry after incarceration and workforce development.

In deconstruction, vacant rowhouses are not torn down in the efficient tri-step of back-hoe, dump truck and landfill. Instead, the historic houses are taken down by hand in much the same way they were originally constructed. Brick by brick, joist by joist. Bricks, marble steps and old timber are sorted, salvaged and cleaned, and then enter the pipeline for restoration and new construction – old materials giving new projects a special Baltimore touch.

The Baltimore non-profit Humanim founded *Details*[20] in 2014 as a social enterprise that performs deconstruction as a non-profit business with a social mission. It creates jobs for people who have difficulty getting hired, a virtual cycle in which people are being empowered, the environment is protected, material and culture are preserved, and a viable business for re-sale is created. In the first 18 months, about 60 houses have been deconstructed – a small seed that has lots of potential in a city facing at least 16,000 vacant rowhouses, many of them slated for demolition, a city that is saddled with high rates of unemployment and poverty, food deserts, health disparities and crime.

Another solution, one that promises job creation; healthy, locally produced food; and the recycling of lands lying fallow, would also have appeal.

Urban farming makes that promise. From beginnings on tiny lots with a few volunteers dabbling in homegrown tomatoes and basil, it has grown into a full-blown urban strategy officially supported by Baltimore's Office of Sustainability, the Baltimore Development Corporation and the Health Department. They actively promote the City's urban agriculture enterprises and everything that goes with it. Can they deliver?

The commitment of city government was clearly on display when *Holly Freishtat*, Baltimore City Food Policy Director, addressed a bus full of conference participants from all over the country in January 2015. The story she had to tell is so good, that even the Associated Press,[21] the US Conference of Mayors and others took notice of Baltimore as a city on the forefront and a city that gets it when it comes to linking food, health, schools and community development, topics that often lead a sad existence in the shadows of glamorous urban projects.

Created as a non-profit and still largely funded by grants, the food section of the Baltimore Planning Department can act like a city agency but shift to the flexibility of a non-profit within the blink of an eye. Freishat collaborates with the Departments of Housing, the Baltimore City School System and the Baltimore Development Corporation to deal specifically with food retail issues. For data she collaborates with the local Johns Hopkins Bloomberg School of Public Health. This collaborative effort called the *Baltimore Food Policy Initiative* attacks inadequate access to healthy food and bad eating habits on many fronts, simultaneously

- by actively promoting city neighborhoods as locations for supermarkets,
- by creating incentive programs for corner stores to carry healthy food choices,
- by bringing healthy food to local residents through a Virtual Supermarket,[22]
- by negotiating local food sourcing with school cafeteria vendors,
- by sending school kids to the farms run by the school system, and
- by designating certain vacant lots or derelict city properties as areas for farming.

Big City Farms is a now defunct Baltimore-based urban farming company intent on building a network of urban farms for job creation and the improvement of vacant and blighted urban land, founded by Winstead Rouse, the son of renowned developer Jim Rouse. Sandtown's "Mayor" Elder C. W. Harris carries the Sandtown farm with 22-foot-wide and 150-foot-long plastic sheds ("hoop houses") with raised hydroponic planting beds of local, organically grown, healthy and sustainable food forth as Strength to Love II. Food is sold to restaurants, institutions, grocers and individual consumers.

Figure 2.13 Strength to Love II urban farm, Sandtown

© Strength to Love II

Sandtown, of course, is the same neighborhood that Rouse's father tried to turn around some 30 years earlier. Strength to Love II occupies 1.5 acres in the backs of rowhouses on lots cleared of vacant rowhouses.

A thousand acres, Ted Rouse believed, could be farmed like this in Baltimore alone, on vacant lots, surplus park space and the like.[23]

Indeed, urban farms are thriving in many places: The *Real Food Farm* in Clifton Park collaborates with *Baltimore Civic Works*, a Johns Hopkins project, which "strengthens Baltimore's communities through education, skills development and community service".[24] In addition, the *Real Food Farm* experiments with specialties such as bee-keeping, composting and soil creation, as well as sharing amenities such as their refrigeration unit and tool sharing.

On the site of a former water pumping station in and among gorgeous industrial buildings now engulfed by decay and weeds rises the *Baltimore Food Hub*, intended to be the crown jewel of urban farming. The hub is to become an incubator for new farmers and food businesses, a community space for education around health and nutrition, and a resource for city planning and food policy development. Ten million dollars of investment are anticipated.

110   *Case studies*

Notes

1 Jesus Leal Trujillo and Joseph Parilla, *Redefining Global Cities*, a publication of the Global Cities Initiative, Brookings Institution, Sept. 2016. www.brookings. edu/wp-content/uploads/2016/09/metro_20160928_gcitypes.pdf

2 Dawn Papadrea, *The 15 Best Cities for Millennial College Students*, Online Colleges Survey, Mar. 3, 2015. www.onlinecolleges.com/rankings/best-cities-for-millennial-college-students.html#methodology

3 Who We Are, *Innovation Village*. www.innovatebaltimore.org/

4 MICA Facts and History, 1824–Today, *Historical Timeline*. www.mica.edu/About_MICA/Facts_and_History/1847-1878_Renewal_and_Expansion_in_the_Industrial_Age.html. Fred Lazarus, *State of the Arts*, video. www.youtube.com/watch?v=dxI-AM0tlDg

5 US News and World Report, *MICA*. www.mica.edu/About_MICA.html, http://grad-schools.usnews.rankingsandreviews.com/best-graduate-schools/top-fine-arts-schools/fine-arts-rankings

6 www.mica.edu/Programs_of_Study/Graduate_Programs/Design_Leadership_(MBAMA).html

7 Maryland State Arts Council, website about *Arts and Entertainment Districts*, Irani and Grimm, *Maryland A/E Districts Impact Analysis*, Towson University, Apr. 2015. www.msac.org/programs/arts-entertainment-districts https://issuu.com/marylandarts/docs/msac_2014_resi_impact_analysis_fina_dd10052c89000a

8 Charlie Duff, *State of the Arts*, video, May 6, 2013. www.youtube.com/watch?v=p7VoDGNxiB4

9 Joseph McNeely, Homewood Community Partners Initiative, *A Call to Action, Findings and Recommendations*, July 2, 2012. www.centralbaltimore.org/wp-content/uploads/2014/01/HCPI-Report-mod-1-2-2013.pdf

10 Author's notes from Central Baltimore Housing Strategy presentation, Baltimore, March 9, 2016.

11 At Open Works, we believe everyone is a maker. We've built a place where anyone can build nearly anything – that's where you come in. www.openworksbmore.com/

12 Morgan Eichensehr, "Open Works maker space will create jobs and hope". *Baltimore Business Journal*, Sept. 20, 2016.

13 Barbara Hopkins, The Path to Baltimore's "Best Prospect" Jobs Without a College Degree, *Abell Foundation Report*, March 2015. www.abell.org/sites/default/files/publications/ed-careercred315.pdf

14 http://beta.fortune.com/fortune500

15 Kevin Plank's Venture Capital adviser Demian Costa, at a presentation to Baltimore Heritage, April 4, 2016. Author's notes from the event.

16 Author's note from an on-site interview with Smalley, July 15, 2016.

17 Edward Ericson, Point of Departure: Imagining a New Future for Sparrows Point, *Baltimore City Paper*, Oct. 17, 2012.

18 New York City Department of Parks and Recreation, *Freshkills Park*. www.nycgovparks.org/park-features/freshkills-park

19 Melody Simmons, Sparrows Point Developer Plots 130 Acre Hotel, Retail Project, *Baltimore Business Journal*, May 24, 2016. www.bizjournals.com/baltimore/blog/real-estate/2016/05/exclusivesparrows-point-developer-plots-150-acre.html?ana=e_du_pub&s=article_du&ed=2016-05-24&u=J%2BHOmx BC%2FdXBdcF5E3a4uA021ee55f&t=1464124826&j=73476842

20 Hunanim Social Enterprise, Every Brick Has a Story. Every Piece of Wood Has a Past. To Our Crew, This Is More Than a Job – It's a Craft, *Details*. www.details.org/

21 Ben Nuckols, Missing Fresh Foods in Baltimore, New Urban Food Czar Aims to Change the Way the City Eats, *NBC News*, July 7, 2010. www.nbcnews.com/id/38132706/ns/health-diet_and_nutrition/%20-%20.VNk5lObF98E#.WAjBSuUrLBQ

22 Baltimore City, *Virtual Supermarket*, Baltimore residents can order groceries online and pick them up at set locations with no registration or delivery fees. Providing access to healthy foods at supermarket prices, especially in neighborhoods where food access is limited, is the goal. The Virtual Supermarket Program is run by the Baltimore City Health Department's Baltimarket program in partnership with ShopRite. www.baltimarket.org/virtual-supermarket/

23 Author's notes from a tour of the farm on January 29, 2015, where Ted Rouse spoke on site about the operations. He has since withdrawn from this operation.

24 Baltimore Civic Works website. https://civicworks.com/about-us/. Civic Works strengthens Baltimore's communities through education, skills development and community service.

Part 3

How to break the cycles

The second unrest gives Baltimore the opportunity to finally get it right, giving national and global trends a local twist.

A legacy city like Baltimore needs to bundle a few of its assets and potentials and market them aggressively to the nomadic creative class and to a global market in which cities become ever stronger forces. Progressive industries have long recognized that their biggest asset is their people. This is also true for cities, but many legacy cities have left entire parts of their population on the sidelines and in deplorable living conditions. A people-based approach controlled by the people and for the people has the potential to unleash a huge potential of energy and creativity.

Understood as a system, city governance must align its many initiatives in favor of sustainable virtuous cycles that propel the system away from the vicious cycles that currently absorb so much energy.

3.1 Brownfield redevelopment

On large former industrial sites, legacy cities can grow, attract game-changing industries and leverage broad community benefits.

What jobs have a future in the Baltimore region? The combination of production, shipping and trade will be around thanks to the port, the industrial heritage and the excellent connectivity to huge markets. In the past, those assets were sufficient to attract industries and workers. In the future, the assets need to be paired with quality of life amenities and urbanity for work, recreation, entertainment and lifelong learning, all areas in which the Baltimore region has much to offer. Two huge former industrial sites are currently well positioned to combine all these aspects.

The larger site is the 3,100-acre former steel site of Sparrows Point peninsula. It could become as formative and influential as the Research Triangle Park in North Carolina once was or the Docklands in London. But it could also just become like everything else in Baltimore County. The old steel site has fantastic deep-water access good for industry and to celebrate water as a resource or a recreational amenity.

> Why not make it great? . . . The one thing I'll tell you is I just want to do great things. I just want to be involved in projects that are great and build things that have people go 'wow.' One of my passions in life is I love blowing people's minds.[1]

Port Covington is the site where Under Armour CEO Kevin Plank wants to demonstrate his ambitions. His desire for "wow" provides a foil for how to design development in general and how to combine work, life and play on a waterfront brownfield. More importantly, the development could also be a trailblazer for a more equitable future. If all goes by the plan that was approved late in 2016, waterfront development won't be used to further accentuate the divide in the city, but to lift six disadvantaged adjacent communities by funding workforce development, providing affordable housing and providing best practice examples for smart and ecological sensible development.

Port Covington's redevelopment began piecemeal. Once home of an innovative coal transfer facility and a big railyard, the first effort of redevelopment resulted in a windowless Walmart overlooking the waterfront – an unmitigated failure of imagination. Big box on the shore was the wrong use in that location, and without a bigger idea for the whole, it led into a dead end. Now, with Sagamore's comprehensive development plan that includes the "global headquarters" of Under Armour and an entire new section of town on the table, there is certainly the "wow".

The planned 266-acre brownfield redevelopment, with 9 to 13 million square feet of possible development and up 14,000 housing units, is bigger than Baltimore's Harbor East, HarborPoint and Canton Crossing combined, all three recent waterfront redevelopment areas. Under Armour's global headquarters alone is with 40 acres about the size of Harbor East and HarborPoint together. The planned 3 million square feet for the headquarters alone are about the same as all the mixed-use development planned for HarborPoint, Baltimore's densest brownfield redevelopment. Port Covington's build-out is supposed to last over 20 to 25 years with a private investment estimated to exceed $5 billion.

Big cities thrive when they can open up centrally located land areas that are not as restricted as the historic center itself. Paris, London, Hamburg and Rotterdam all have their expansion areas in which innovative design can unfold without threatening the identity of the city as it has come to be known over centuries. Under Armour and its Sagamore development arm showed the Baltimore City design review panel all the right things without a City-imposed framework of rules: green development, public access, walkability, transit, bikeways, public parks, mixed use, mixed-income housing and waterfront promenades are all included in the masterplan designed by Elkus Manfredi Architects of Boston. Sagamore explains its thrive for innovation and excellence this way: "We want the best people in the world to work here".

The plan was presented a year after the unrest. Platitudes of "the rising tide that lifts all boats" or trickle-down theories, often employed to justify developments that chiefly serve the well-to-do, wouldn't do this time. When Under Armour asked for more than $600 million of tax increment financing (TIF) bonds for infrastructure construction, it rekindled the downtown versus neighborhoods debate in full force, which is a discussion that goes on in many other legacy cities.

When it looked like the city administration would just wave the new development right through and approve the TIF bonds without much scrutiny, BUILD, the church coalition that in the early 1990s had masterminded the plans of rebuilding Baltimore's poor community of Sandtown, stepped up. Unimpressed by the "wow factor", it greeted the Port Covington plans with hostility and the exclamation "Here we go again!", referencing *the two Baltimores*: the glitz concentrated along the waterfront and the poverty in the inner-city neighborhoods. BUILD, housing advocates and unions mobilized

Figure 3.1 Port Covington rendering of the final build-out

© Sagamore Developments

hundreds of residents and workers to fight the TIF bond approval in hearings of the City Council. The noisy protest strategy paid off. Under Armour's delegates sat down for a new round of negotiations directly with various activist groups, with Council members acting as facilitators and with the Baltimore Development Corporation.

Plank's big gesture could signal a watershed moment for Baltimore's future in which the city could get over its inferiority complex, raise local standards and get anchored with Under Armour as a corporation that could employ as many as 10,000 people locally. Sustainable city renaissance cannot be done any longer from the top down using a trickle-down philosophy. The negotiations finally brought what the community had fought for in the 1990 American Can struggle: impact fees in the shape of one of the largest community benefits agreements ever conceived anywhere, including $100 million in direct payments (such as $39 million in benefits for the neighboring communities, $25 million for workforce training, $10 million for no-interest loans and additional support to minority-owned businesses and start-ups and guaranteeing prevailing wage rates for all infrastructure construction) and $35 million worth of privately acquired land that will be turned back to the public with unrestricted public access. Maybe most important: The company commits to ensuring 20 per cent of all housing units are affordable across all income brackets from 80 percent AMI down. Forty per cent of the required affordable units can be provided off site, which is potentially an important technique to spread the investment into disinvested communities.

Whether everything will come to pass quite as progressively as it was presented remains to be seen. There is a substantial risk that a 40-year plan does not unfold as envisioned. It is likely that Under Armour will complete their new headquarters and the waterfront infrastructure and roadways. If those investments can unlock demand to build out all parcels as envisioned, it would likely shift Baltimore into growth mode. Port Covington is Baltimore's best shot yet to capture a sizable chunk of the regional growth and direct it into the city, and it is also an experiment in building a new kind of manufacturing industry.

Tradepoint Atlantic and Under Armour's Port Covington must be seen together. The sports apparel newcomer already has a stake in both sites. The "wow" and the equity achieved in Port Covington could be the blueprint for a future that could influence the entire Boston to Washington megalopolis and place Baltimore as an important player. The sites prove that growth can happen in an inelastic city and without sprawl. For this to occur, though, Baltimore City and County would have to truly collaborate.

Note

1 Under Armour CEO Kevin Plank in an Interview with the *Baltimore Business Journal*, March 2, 2015.

3.2 Transportation

Legacy cities will benefit the most from the next transportation revolution.

Baltimore's transit system is currently holding the city back. The case study of the Baltimore Red Line shows how much modern transit has become a political football of politicians in much the same way as high-speed rail in the United States has become one on the national stage. But sometimes being behind can be an opportunity to jump to the head of the line.

An example is Baltimore's bike-share system. Installed in the fall of 2016, it is late by any measure, but it comes with a new twist: Baltimore's fleet has 50 per cent electric-assist power bicycles, a novelty in the United States. This feature will make bike-sharing mainstream beyond bicycle enthusiasts and open the possibility of becoming a true "last-mile" transport solution with a much lower fitness entry threshold than a standard bike.

The biggest game changer yet will be the autonomous vehicle (AV). Already entering the stage of mobility options, it can make traditional transportation failings even more dramatic, but it could also mitigate them, depending on how the future unfolds. AVs could reenergize sprawl and further suck energy from cities, just as streetcars did and then the automobile. That frightening scenario is likely if AVs remain privately owned and continue to be used the same way as the automobile today. AVs would only enlarge the tolerable commuting distance by reducing congestion, increasing travel speeds and making time spent in the vehicle more tolerable.

Alternatively, with the right policies in place and if AVs facilitate the insight that autos are poor investments that sit idle more than 90 per cent of the time, AVs can be a huge boost for cities. If users shift to mobility via fleet vehicle, a better future could emerge in which the AV would bring about the ultimate victory of Jane Jacobs over Robert Moses. Rechargeable electric emission-free vehicles used on a per-need base won't require a garage at home or parking deck at work. Fleet vehicles would provide mobility in a much more efficient manner. As much as one-third of the urban space currently devoted to the automobile could be repurposed from parking, gas stations and extra-wide roadways to higher and better uses. The urban fleet

AV would blur the line between individual transportation and transit and improve the current standing of transit. Transit providers could focus on operating high-volume trunk lines by whatever mode they currently use, while the dispersal and last-mile transportation could be handled by demand-based AV micro transit. Eventually, with automated buses and trains, transit operations themselves could become vastly more economical to operate, allowing high-frequency service on trunk lines in many more places.

Legacy cities that have been fighting air quality problems and congestion would become much more livable and healthier places. Baltimore, which was initially laid out with the density suitable for walking, horses and streetcars with small blocks and a redundant walkable street network, is much more likely to reap great benefits from the AV revolution than the sprawling sunbelt cities that were designed around the car.

3.3 Making and innovation

The new economy lowers the entry threshold for people whose creativity and energy were previously excluded.

How technology shifts the economic base and how things are made, what skills are needed and how people will make a living can assist comeback cities to include their marginalized populations. Diversity, collaboration, flexibility, creativity, knowledge and openness are requirements of the postindustrial economy and the places having those attributes in their DNA are cities. Those cities that perform best in these categories will be the leaders of tomorrow. Or as Richard Florida states, "startups and high-tech industry have become urban".[1]

Entrenched poverty fosters immobility and a startling reduction of choices resulting in pathologies that affect the individual as well as the community. Unfortunately, cities are also hotbeds of those characteristics. No city will thrive if significant parts of its population are locked up, literally or figuratively. Societies who write off whole segments of their own people, whether they are women, gays, religious minorities or people of color, can't perform well in the economy of tomorrow. Engaging disadvantaged populations to the best of their abilities is a global challenge. Richard May co-founded the Baltimore Innovation Village with exactly the purpose of engaging the majority of city residents in mind. Continuing an economy without the majority who are people of color would be like "the Baltimore Ravens playing with just three players on the field", as May told me.[2]

Traditional workforce development tries to connect undereducated individuals with low-paying jobs, which are often outside of the community where people live and for businesses that don't invest in the community and often offer jobs that have no future. Innovation Village Baltimore works on engaging disadvantaged communities in those drivers that will define the future of work. Likely such engagement will not take place in the typical employment at the bottom of the wage scale working outside the community with assets accruing in somebody else's pocket. Rather, this engagement happens with service providers, start-ups and entrepreneurs that build assets and social strength right in their community. Untapping the energy and creativity in a youth that has found no access to traditional industries and giving a helping hand to those who want to thrive is a winning and necessary strategy and the best investment a city can make. Many businesses and universities recognize this and are partnering with Innovation Village.

How can poor people lacking formal education step out of their exclusion? The answer lies within the same shifts that eliminated well-paying stable jobs but are also providing the opportunity of the future. Education is no longer exclusively a matter of a degree achieved in the first 22 or so years of life; not only does learning have to become a lifelong exercise, but the definition of what is considered skill and knowledge also needs to be a continually moving target providing opportunities for entry throughout life. Increasingly, jobs will require social, emotional and creative intelligence and entrepreneurial thinking instead of simple formal knowledge. This promises the participation of many more people than the old order of work could productively employ.

The key element of what some call derisively the "gig economy" is the relatively open access for people with all kinds of skills. The informal economy is in many ways much more treacherous than the steel job at Bethlehem Steel with what were considered guaranteed good wages, 40-hour workweeks, benefits and pensions, but the threshold for entry is much lower. It is easy to engage and disengage, whether part time, full time, in combination with other jobs or with learning or family obligations.

The biggest benefit of the Uber transportation model is not the ease of use for riders, but the ease with which people with a car can leverage that possession to make money.

In Baltimore, the spontaneously hired non-licensed driver, the "hack", is a longstanding practice. Compared to it, driving for Uber or Lyft is a big step up in terms of safety, predictability and income, even though Uber as a global corporation isn't necessarily focused on driver well-being.

The start-up culture nurtured by the Baltimore Innovation Village is not asking for large government programs to lift poor communities, but aims at the entrepreneurial spirit of young unemployed people to use their skills by providing the services that are needed in their communities in new and creative ways. Their learning is done by doing, and the wealth is accumulated where it is created. Having a car or an apartment or house (Airbnb) are still significant entry thresholds, yet a small enterprise is possible without formal degrees. Sidewalk cooks can hone their skills legally in kitchen incubators sprouting all over Baltimore. Simpler, not necessarily high-tech work can be available in food production, deconstruction of rowhouses or recycling. Tool libraries and maker spaces lower the capital cost for people with more ideas than money, especially if they are funded by angel investors or local companies that need a steady flow of creatives to join their ranks. A renaissance of values such as craft and product authenticity can and should allow a brighter future for those who want to practice traditional skills, whether it is food production, construction, furniture or cooking.

There may well be too much hype around the *sharing economy*,[3] but there is no doubt that start-ups, maker spaces, funding pitches and angel investors are important elements in the journey of finding new ways to work and make a living. This culture is coming to Baltimore later than it came to Seattle or Austin, but instead of appealing to only the creative "know-mades", Baltimore can differentiate itself by pivoting towards its impoverished communities. First steps have been taken from within and from the outside. Jeff Cherry came to Baltimore from New York to attract and fund "conscious capital" with his Conscious Venture Labs. His goal is to invest in 300 Baltimore companies in five years.

Large companies and institutions such as Johns Hopkins University or Blueprint Robotics engage with disadvantaged communities by employing staff through *re-entry programs* such as *Turnaround Tuesday*,[4] organized by the same BUILD coalition that partnered in the early Sandtown investments and emerged once again as the voice of the unheard.

The critique of the "gig economy" as a neoliberal glorification of the entrepreneur who, as a pseudo independent individual, has to hustle for "gigs" to make a living is justified and has a prominent voice in Baltimore as well. Johns Hopkins political science professor Lester Spence has expressed his skepticism about the pitch that everyone can be an entrepreneur in his book *Knocking the Hustle*.[5]

Notes

1 Richard Florida, The Rise of the Urbanpreneur, How the Internet Ushered in a New Era, *The Atlantic CityLab*, Oct. 20, 2016. www.citylab.com/work/2016/10/rise-of-the-urbanpreneur/504434/?utm_source=nl__link3_102016
2 Klaus Philipsen, Interview With Richard May, *Community Architect Daily*, June 14, 2016.
3 Sarah Kessler, The Sharing Economy Is Dead, *Fast Economy*, Sept. 2015. www.fastcompany.com/3050775/the-sharing-economy-is-dead-and-we-killed-it
4 *BUILD*. www.buildiaf.org/2016/04/johns-hopkins-25-corporations-commit-blocal/
5 Lester Spence, *Knocking the Hustle, Against the Neoliberal Turn in Black Politics*, Punctum Books, 2015. https://punctumbooks.com/titles/knocking-the-hustle/
   Bret Mc Cabe, Lester Spence Argues that African-Americans Have Bought Into the Wrong Politics, *Johns Hopkins Magazine*, Winter 2015. https://hub.jhu.edu/magazine/2015/winter/lester-spence-african-americans-neoliberalism/

3.4 Crowd-based production

Open-source design outpaces traditional product development and allows customization to replace mass production.

The new economy is already here. Architects and city planners should pay attention to the disruptions of the traditional way of how things are designed or made as a matter of survival. While homeowners or developers likely won't soon start designing or making their own houses, offices or shopping centers with 3-D printers, crowd-based design and 3-D production will be part of the third industrial revolution that will be around for a while and will change just about everything in a way not yet predictable. Only small seeds are visible, be it at the e-NABLE conference with its prosthetic limbs at Johns Hopkins or at local start-ups and maker spaces. Baltimore is just gearing up to be a relevant part of the future.

The future of 3-D printing, just like the sharing economy, is dismissed by many as more hype than substance. True, its usefulness is still emerging. It has always been that way. When the Wright brothers took flight, people wondered what the noisy contraption could possibly be good for, and looking at their plane today one would have to concede they had a point. When personal computers came out a mere 35 or so years ago, many people asked the same question since computers were only known for doing long and complicated computations of the kind nobody needed to do at home. Early home computers had anemic powers, were cumbersome to boot up and even gifted people struggled to come up with ideas on what to do with them. They programmed little green figures for their kids in what became the first computer games. Today, the applications of that little computer in our pocket are so numerous that we can't even imagine life without it. Today's 3-D printers look as cumbersome as an old Ataris computer, and people struggle again to find better uses than printing napkin rings, phone cases, or sculptures of their own heads.

But those homemade custom phone cases keep Chinese manufacturers up at night. Their mass-produced, globally distributed product won't remain competitive if people can make a customized version in their own basement and save the shipping. That will make shippers sleepless, too – less trucking, less air cargo, less road space and fewer cartons. In the quick churn of development, workers in the huge FedEx distribution center that replaced the plant where General Motors used to produce Astro Vans may soon face replacement by robots. But the robots still need to be made and programmed.

Even if these changes happen incrementally and in partial markets, they will recast the physical world. Baltimore's port specialization in general cargo may have just been a bet on the right horse, if one equates containers as symbols of mass production and general cargo as customization.

If custom production instead of serial production is the new way of making things, the economic theories of the long-dead economist Schumpeter can finally be buried for good. His theories were built around the need for concentration of capital for huge investments on machines of mass production that allow the *economy of scale*. In a new paradigm everybody must not only be an inventor, but also a producer. Goodbye assembly line, goodbye factory floor, goodbye logistics industry, goodbye "just in time" shipping. Goodbye to the large corporations that manage the complicated set-up from product development to production, goodbye to the big overhead that comes from the inefficiencies of big corporations that are only so big and unwieldy because the infrastructure needed to produce in mass is so exorbitantly expensive. Goodbye merger mania – big isn't needed anymore. Goodbye bankers and financiers; the future doesn't cost much more than a 3-D printer and some spools of materials. Hello to the masses that had been shut out from production and finally can become part of the game again.

This wildly exaggerated depiction of the future shows technological opportunities for engaging the unemployed and underemployed that the industrial era has left behind en masse.

Of course, not everything can be produced in those magic printers, and not everything needs to be custom. There will always be mass production, "subtractive" fabrication or mold injection, and maybe biologically inspired new ways of making.

Still, already now the high cost of prototypes, injection molds or extrusion dies for mass production can be lowered drastically through 3-D printing, allowing more product variation for less cost. Some complicated shapes in hydro plants or airplane turbines can already be repaired by using the additive printing process. It doesn't take much imagination to see that the crowd-produced prosthetics can be used as attachments for robots to make them cheaper and more versatile.

When making things in our own four walls becomes as commonplace as consulting and document printing from home, we will have a better idea about the social, political and physical implications of this revolution and what it will mean for design, buildings, cities, transportation and the future of a legacy city like Baltimore that never got around to fully separate its uses as much as the suburbs, as America's sunbelt cities or China's giant new towns.

Based on the time it took to get from the Apple 2e computer to the iPhone, there won't be very much time to plan for the future in which people are once again not only consumers but also makers, where place matters all day and where people aren't quarantined from nine to five any longer. A future that could bring an expectation of quality replaces the sameness of quantity.

Not all changes in making things will be high tech. Some trends point towards low-tech and highly labor-intensive crafts. Urban agriculture takes up the challenge of bringing food closer to the globally growing urban population in experimental ways, trying out new ways of low-impact production and the integration of urban surfaces into food production. The hoop houses in Baltimore's Sandtown are just a simple beginning. Vertical farming included in office tower façades, green roof farming on distribution warehouses and "edible parks" will be next and can contribute to job creation, reduction of food insecurity and better health and may solve many of the environmental issues associated with current farming and current construction practices.

3.5 Staging a comeback

A sustainable comeback requires inclusion. By aligning efforts, Baltimore can be tipped into a virtuous cycle.

Decline can be final, but it can become a precursor for a comeback. Nations, corporations and cities have demonstrated the potential dialectic embedded in decline in which a liability can be turned into an asset. *From Rustbelt to Brainbelt* suggests such a dialectic reversal. From a city management perspective, how can a negative trajectory be actually reversed? Physics suggests that reversal, which means stopping and going backward, requires a lot of energy. Few rustbelt cities have actually managed to shift from decline to growth, but some prove that it is possible, most notably Columbus, Ohio. Baltimore, located in one of the most prosperous urban conglomerations of the entire world, can stage more than stagnation.

In cities like Baltimore, whose budget depends to a large part on property and payroll piggyback taxes, population growth is a key metric that influences most other metrics of prosperity and well-being. Baltimore's good news is that in spite of strong differences on the neighborhood level, on average, population loss has come to a halt for some years now. The large and growing cohort of the elderly is an ideal candidate for the repopulation of legacy cities. So far, the split between the shrinking legacy cities in the rustbelt and the growing sunbelt cities is replicated with the elderly: In rustbelt cities, the proportion of folks 65 and older is declining in spite of their growing proportion in the overall population. Only in sunbelt regions is the growth of the elderly population similar in the core and the region. Legacy cities usually have excellent universities, great libraries, parks, famous hospitals and a very walkable layout with relatively decent public transport, all factors that can be leveraged to attract the elderly. They don't mind that urban schools are not always on par; they won't crowd classrooms, nor will they drive excessively. The demographics of aging present an opportunity for Baltimore along with immigrants, refugees and millennials.

Times of a fragile balance can become pivotal as a *fork in the road* or a *watershed moment* when several metrics are synchronized just the right way to create the small momentum that is needed for tipping. In what physicists call phase-transition, an entire system can reach a point of transition from one state to another, for example when cold water suddenly gels to become ice or when vapor turns into a torrential downpour. Positive or negative feedback loops can become run-away cycles, good or bad.

If disparities within the system are too large, the city as a system cannot reach the transition point even if macro trends such as the national economy or the renaissance of cities are favorable. The drag of the failing metrics, whether it is too much crime, poor education or poor health outcomes is too big. Catastrophic events, such as Baltimore's unrest and the renewed national debate about racial inequality, tend to unite disparate forces around similar efforts and propel a city forward. The Baltimore unrest enforced the insight among institutions, universities and private stakeholders that it is in their self-interest to engage with populations and neighborhoods left behind so far.

Where many forces are engaged in halting downward spirals, real progress can be made. For example, Baltimore's infant mortality rate: In African American neighborhoods, it was slashed in half in only seven years.[1]

But the city cannot solve its problems alone. While the sprawl combating efforts of Maryland's governors, including previous mayors of Baltimore, were certainly designed to help Baltimore, land preservation and revitalization were the drivers rather than equity or social justice. A city that is attracting young people from around the nation because of its opportunities will allow the region another look at taking a fair share in caring for the less fortunate and reinstating a social compact on a regional level because most suburbs cannot thrive on their own either.

The unrest has brought these interdependencies into bright focus. Attracting more affluent residents to a revitalized city is certainly a necessary strategy, but it must be accompanied by constructing affordable-housing social services in the entire region. Only fair burden sharing can bring down the tax disparity between the core city and the surrounding jurisdictions from the current level in which city residents pay twice the property tax of most county residents. Burden sharing, too, would create a virtuous feedback loop with a vital core city as the driver for the entire region.

Embedded in a nationwide economic recovery, Baltimore is at a tipping point. The new Mayor coming into office at the beginning of 2017 will have the opportunity to move the needle in the right direction. It takes only subtle but strategic intervention. In housing, revitalization, transportation, production and innovation, Baltimore already has momentum and can create virtuous cycles that pull other metrics up as well. The national and global trends of work and production, knowledge and creativity and the importance of good quality of life can support Baltimore's comeback.

Note

1 Baltimore City Health Department, *Baltimore City Experiences Record Low Infant Mortality Rate in 2015*, Press Release, Oct. 5, 2016. http://health.baltimorecity. gov/news/press-releases/2016-10-05-baltimore-city-experiences-record-low-infant-mortality-rate-2015

Conclusion
Globalization, localization and cities

Cities will remain important players in global relations with innovations in production and transportation, legacy cities have a leg up.

Cities or, more precisely, *metropolitan areas* have been beacons of trade, exchange, globalization, openness and collaboration forever. Cities have gained importance from the fading relevance of nation-states. The US legacy cities of New York, Philadelphia and Baltimore have historically experienced the benefit of openness and diversity as the once official ports of entry for a steady flow of immigrants into the United States. At times fear has brought restrictions, such as the strongly racially tainted Immigration Act of 1924, which sought to curb Italian, Jewish and Asian immigrants in favor of Germans and Nordic states. Immigration provided fuel to the legacy cities just as it does for today's new sunbelt metros from Miami to San Diego and Los Angeles.

Yet, once again, fear dominates the debate, even though in today's global metro centers the language is English, the code is from Microsoft or Apple, and the means of communication and networking can be found under globally identical applications developed in the United States. Given the strong dominance of the United States in information technology, it is curious that so many in this country should feel so threatened by globalization.

Citizens around the world believe that "other" countries are the winners in globalization. The deeper cause for the discontent is a crisis of legitimacy in which control has slipped away from nation-states to global corporations and where trade rules are adjudicated by bodies that are not controlled and overseen by democratically elected representatives. People do not feel properly represented and see their own fate and that of their country as a play-ball of global forces and supranational alliances. Global migration caused by war, suppression and inequitable distribution of opportunity plays into the fear. The response is withdrawal and identification with turf, a trend some call localization or tribalization.

Cities are where the world's business, financial and human capital are concentrated. Cities are also where the world's population is increasingly concentrated, and they are the primary source of growth and innovation. They are also the leading consumers of energy and the primary source of greenhouse gasses.[1]

As such, cities are well positioned to reconcile the need for international trade with the challenge of political representation. Should nations become even less able than now to collaborate on the big global challenges of climate change and water, nimble cities can take on much of the international collaboration as they have already done in the case of the Green Cities Initiative.

Thus, localization can be a threat and a benefit to cities. Cities such as Calais, Vienna and Munich, not national governments, have received, housed, clothed and fed the waves of immigrants and refugees. The wars of the world have been carried into cities, almost regardless of their location. Cities more than states have actually solved the daily problems. They are the understandable and manageable entities with which people can identify. Clearly, cities and metro areas have their own issues of legitimate and equitable representation, especially when it comes to regional collaboration, but urban areas are the best answer for the need to feel a sense of representation and belonging. Cities still offer direct interaction with authority.

The risk is highlighted by the discussions about London's future as a global center after the British vote for exit from the EU. Nationalism can make it harder for cities to act as global partners and beneficiaries of free trade. But when nations become gridlocked and barely able to join or approve international agreements of any kind, whether it is in knowledge exchange, partnerships, trade or climate action, an opportunity opens up for cities. As the most identifiable mile markers in the geospatial landscape, they jump into the breach and act where nations don't. As Neil Peirce recognized in his book *Citistates*, metro areas can once again become the places where international and national forces interact just as they have in the city-states of the middle ages.

Instant communication and information will continue to make the world flat.[2] Products, trends and cultures will continue to become more similar. Legacy cities can absorb some of the tribal energy in a productive way. In a world of continued homogenization, legacy cities with their authenticity, grit and strong resident loyalty are strong brands and cultural identifiers, for which the identification with the metropolitan sport teams is just one representation.

Taking this type of thinking a step further, it is conceivable that Rotterdam, London, Frankfurt, Stockholm and Lisbon begin to pick up the pieces after the shock of Britain's Brexit vote and reduce the impact of new national isolation through metropolitan collaboration.

In that world where global cities become global players, the Baltimore metro region, which is not only located in one of only a dozen or so global metropolitan clusters, but also right next door to the capital of world's most powerful nation, is well positioned to play a role for a long time to come.

Notes

1 Global Green Cities of the 21st Century, *Why Green Cities*. http://globalgreencities. com/why-green-cities/
2 Thomas Friedman, *The World is Flat*, Picador, 2007. In the book *The World Is Flat 3.0* the author presents "an essential update on globalization, its opportunities for individual empowerment, its achievements at lifting millions out of poverty, and its environmental, social, and political drawbacks". Author's website: www.thomaslfriedman.com/the-world-is-flat-3-0/

Index